T0108536

Home-made
CHEESE

Home-made
CHEESE

Cheesemaking made simple

PAUL THOMAS

Photographs by William Shaw

LORENZ BOOKS

Contents

INTRODUCTION

Success in cheesemaking is dependent on the quality of the raw materials and the ability of the cheesemaker to best understand and compensate for subtle variations in the composition of the milk used. These factors, as well as the impact of using milk from different species, are described in this chapter, along with the role of starter cultures, rennet and salt; not just in terms of the function they have during the make but also with regard to their continuing influence during ripening.

We will also look at the equipment available to the home cheesemaker, including some do-it-yourself alternatives, and address some of the issues relating to food safety in cheesemaking, such as the importance of effective cleaning and disinfection.

In addition to understanding the ingredients from which cheese is made, the chapter explores the processes that influence the transformation of milk to curd and then mature cheese, providing the home cheesemaker with a broad level of background information, which can be applied when trying out the recipes.

The Cheesemaking Process

Although there is an incredible range of different cheeses produced across the world, the processes involved with making them can be remarkably similar. Up until the point that the curds are heated and stretched, the means by which the extremely elastic mozzarella is made is not so very different from that of Cheddar cheese which, in turn, shares some similarities in production with crumbly Cheshire cheese.

THE BASIC PRINCIPLES

For most recipes, the milk is heated, usually to 30–32°C/86–90°F but sometimes as high as 36°C/97°F and sometimes as low as 21°C/70°F. Starter cultures are then added. These are a mixture of lactic acid bacteria (LAB) that will ferment the sugars in the milk and produce lactic acid. The acidity of cheese helps to prevent the growth of harmful bacteria.

Rennet is stirred in to coagulate the milk. Traditionally an enzyme obtained from the fourth stomach of a calf, kid or lamb, today a substitute suitable for vegetarians may sometimes be used. The rennet causes structural changes to the casein (milk protein) that makes them join together and form a solid curd, a jelly-like network that traps the milk's water content and fat within it. The process typically takes 30 minutes to 2 hours.

The subsequent cutting of the coagulated curd increases the surface-area-to-volume ratio, making it easier for the water trapped in the curd to then be expelled in the form of whey, a mixture of water and whey proteins. The amount of moisture lost can be carefully controlled by cutting the curd more or less finely, stirring it to a greater or lesser degree, and possibly heating or 'scalding' the curds.

At a certain point – determined by time, acidity level or the judgement of an experienced cheesemaker – the whey is carefully drained off and the curds may then be placed into moulds to continue draining as they acidify.

Most soft cheeses, which always have high moisture contents, are not cut finely, stirred continuously or scalded – all of which would cause more whey to be lost from the curds than if these things were not done. After the drainage period, these cheeses are usually dry-salted but some varieties are brined.

Semi-hard cheeses, such as Raclette, Tomme de Savoie and some young Gouda cheeses, tend to be cut finely, stirred continuously, packed into moulds and lightly pressed. The cheeses are usually brined but may be dry-salted.

For some hard cheeses such as Cheddar cheese, the curds may be scalded to just below 40°C/104°F before the whey is drained. Curds are allowed to mat together before being cut into blocks, and are stacked to improve whey drainage while the acidification takes place: a process referred to as 'Cheddaring'. Once a specified target acidity has been reached, the blocks are shredded in a curd mill – a series of rotating pegs that break the curds into small pieces – or they can be milled by hand. Salt is mixed into the curds, which are packed into a cloth-lined mould, placed on a cheese-press and pressed overnight.

left **The cheesemaking process involves transforming milk from a liquid into a dazzling plethora of different cheeses.**

For other hard and extra-hard cheeses, such as Grana-type cheeses like Parmigiano Reggiano, curds may be cut down to rice-sized grains and stirred vigorously while they are scalded or 'cooked' to a very high temperature of around 55°C/131°F. The curds are then moulded and the cheeses are pressed and brined before they are matured for a long period of time – up to several years in some cases – during which time they lose a considerable amount of moisture.

THE ROLE OF ACIDIFICATION AND DRAINAGE

To fully understand the influence that each production method has on the finished cheese, we need to consider the combined influence of acidification and drainage. In addition to preventing the growth of pathogens, curd acidification also has an

above **The quality of the pasture on which dairy cows graze is of vital importance to the end product, milk, and the cheese that is subsequently made from it.**

below **Once coagulated, curds for some hard cheeses may be cut finely or scalded to improve drainage. Some are milled, which improves the salt uptake.**

important and sometimes rather overlooked role in the textural development of the cheese. At the pH of fresh milk, about 6.60, the casein (milk protein) is associated with a considerable amount of calcium. It may be helpful to think of calcium as a kind of elastic glue holding together the casein molecules. If the curd is moulded and drained at a high pH, as is the case with Emmental and Reblochon, more calcium will be retained in the curd, conferring the property of elasticity to the finished cheese. As the acidification proceeds, more of the calcium is displaced, allowing

USES FOR WHEY

A by-product of the cheesemaking process, whey is a protein-rich liquid that has many uses, depending on whether or not it is salted.

• Salted whey can be used in place of water for making stocks, breads or savoury pastry – don't add further salt.
• Unsalted whey can be added to smoothies and other drinks or drunk on its own; it is sometimes used to make ricotta; and in the garden it can lower the pH of soil and help to treat powdery mildew.

it to drain off with the whey. So at the other end of the scale, the lactic cheeses moulded at pH 4.60 have lost a significant amount of calcium by the start of drainage and, in the absence of elastic connections, the cheese becomes brittle and crumbly.

A cheese such as Brie can fall somewhere in the middle, between the brittle lactic cheese and the elasticity of something like Reblochon. As a result, achieving the desired consistency can be quite difficult. The curd is often moulded above 6.00, a relatively high pH, but the curds are usually quite large and do not drain particularly well. During the long, slow drainage, the curd acidification allows for the loss of more calcium, resulting in a cheese with textural properties neither as brittle as the lactic cheeses nor as elastic as the Reblochon. The trick to cheesemaking successfully is getting that balance exactly right for each individual cheese.

I like to teach my cheesemaking students by exploring the possibilities of what can go wrong; if we understand the two extreme worst cases then we are better able to feel our way towards the balanced centre ground. Thus, continuing with the example of Brie, let us say that we have a recipe that usually turns out 'perfect' cheeses but that one day the acidification is occurring a bit too fast. If we cut the curd to the 'normal' size and texture, during drainage they will end up shedding more calcium than is usual, making for more brittle or chalky cheeses. Cutting the curds more finely or stirring them a bit more on this occasion would help to correct this by causing more whey to drain off earlier. If the acidification is a bit sluggish, however, then you should do the opposite: don't cut the curds so finely and don't stir quite so frequently.

above left **The amount of calcium that is contained in the whey that is drained from the curds determines the elasticity of the finished cheese.**

above right **Maturing cheeses in varying conditions according to type improves their flavour and can have an effect on their texture, too.**

Let us imagine that, having got the recipe right a few times, the cheesemaker decides to experiment with a new milk supply, switching to rich Jersey cow's milk, for instance. The acidification proceeds according to plan but the cheeses still end up being chalky in the core. It is likely that the increased proportion of fat in the milk is impeding the drainage of the whey. This problem is one of poor drainage rather than fast acidification but the textural outcome is the same. The recipe may be adjusted by cutting the curd more finely and stirring more.

THE BIOCHEMISTRY OF CHEESE-RIPENING

For many cheeses, the actual production process is only a very small part of the timeline from milk to finished product. Fresh curd tastes of very little: slightly sour or with a milky sweetness. The complex flavours of a ripened cheese – whether hard or soft, internally or surface ripened – can thus only be fully realized by maturing the cheese for the appropriate amount of time in specific temperature- and humidity-controlled conditions.

Over the course of time, the casein begins to break down into long and intermediate peptides, then shorter peptides, and finally amino acids, which are the precursor to many of the flavour compounds we find in mature cheeses. This process, called proteolysis, is carried out by natural milk enzymes, such as plasmin, as well as retained rennet, the enzymes of LAB and those of the ripening cultures, whether added intentionally or not.

WHAT IS A SEMI-SOFT CHEESE?

Cheese descriptions are defined according to moisture and fat content in the *1978 General Standard for Cheese* by the Codex Alimentarius Commission of the World Health Organization and the United Nations' Food and Agriculture Organization.

The classifications are: soft, firm/semi-hard, hard and extra-hard. Before reclassification in 1978, the firm/semi-hard category had been subdivided into 'semi-hard' and 'semi-soft'. The latter is a word that has never really gone away; perhaps it is simply too good a description for the texture of cheeses such as Reblochon (seen here) and Raclette, which hover somewhere on the edges of the soft and firm/semi-hard categories.

The term semi-soft is often wrongly used to describe cheeses that are actually soft, which is indicative of the widespread confusion over its use and legal status. To be strictly accurate, the correct term for a semi-soft cheese is 'firm/semi-hard'.

The process of lipolysis (fat breakdown), tends to be less significant to the ripening of most cheese varieties although it plays an important role in the flavour development of some goat's cheeses, blue cheeses and long-aged Parmesan. Excessive lipolysis is sometimes encountered as a spoilage defect, causing rancidity in cheese through the release of free fatty acids, which can be strongly flavoured and impart goaty, peppery, sweaty or soapy taints.

THE CAUSES OF BITTERNESS IN CHEESE

Although proteolysis is desirable for flavour development, it can pose something of a problem. When the formation of peptides from casein occurs faster than they can be broken down into amino acids, bitter peptides can accumulate at levels above the threshold at which they can be tasted. Underlying causes include: an excessive dose of starter or rennet; rennet retained by drainage at low pH; or high levels of plasmin in milk from mastitic animals.

CHEESE TYPE BY RIPENING METHOD AND RIND TREATMENT

Cheese type	Ripening method	Cheese category	Rind treatment	Examples
Unripened/ fresh cheese	n/a	soft	n/a	curd cheese queso fresco
Whey cheese	n/a	soft	n/a	ricotta
Cheeses in brine	n/a	soft	n/a	feta
Ripened cheese	internal ripening	hard cheeses	natural rind larded cloth plasticoat or waxed rind	Tomme de Savoie traditional Cheddar Gouda
			vacuum-packed (no rind)	block Cheddar
		internally mould-ripened (blue)		Stilton Gorgonzola Roquefort
	surface ripening	smear-ripened or washed-rind		Livarot Époisses de Bourgogne Taleggio
		mould-ripened		Brie Camembert

Equipping the Home Dairy

The home dairy comes in many shapes and sizes – from a standard kitchen in which the odd weekend-batch of mozzarella or pat of butter is made, to bags of curd draining and cheeses maturing in a discreet corner, right the way up to a fully equipped amateur dairy tucked away in the garage. The equipment and space needed is dictated only by the ambition of the home cheesemaker and the extent to which they are prepared to let their hobby take over their life. Be warned: cheesemaking can be a fairly compelling pastime.

WHERE TO MAKE CHEESE

That it is possible to make cheese to a very high standard at home cannot be disputed. There are many examples of garage-based cheesemakers – slowly perfecting both their cheeses and their technique with a view to one day setting up a commercial dairy – and some of the best cheeses on the market began life as a home cheesemaking experiment in a bucket or a pan.

At its most basic level, cheesemaking requires an uncluttered space that can easily be cleaned, in a room that can easily be kept warm. As a general rule, if the room is too cold for the cheesemaker to be able to walk around in a T-shirt, it is too cold for the cheese; cool temperatures can inhibit the drainage of whey from the curd and can slow the activity of some of the lactic acid bacteria. Although generally warmer, a family kitchen can be a hub of activity and since many of the makes require long acidification or coagulation, it would be sensible to pick a space where you can work uninterrupted and where the cheeses won't get in the way.

Wherever you find yourself making cheese, it is important that you wash the work surfaces with hot soapy water and disinfect them before use. Hairnets and overcoats are perhaps a bit much for most home cheesemakers; in large-scale food manufacturing, these are used to protect food from contamination by clothes and hair, but at home a clean apron, tying up hair and washing hands will help prevent some cross-contamination. (A dirty apron, however, may actually be worse than no apron at all.)

CHEESEMAKING EQUIPMENT

Buckets and containers The recipes in this book require up to 11.4 litres/3 US gallons of milk, so pans and buckets used for cheesemaking need to be big enough to hold this volume. During the production of lactic cheeses in France it is common to use a *bac de caillage* (coagulation tub), usually with a capacity of about 50 litres/13.2 US gallons. Strong food-grade plastic containers, which are usually readily available, make a suitable substitute, but avoid brittle plastics. Many of the softer cheeses in this book can be made in a food-grade plastic bucket that can hold 15–20 litres/4–5.25 US gallons, so

right **You can buy a curd-draining bag or use a sterilized pillowcase.**

below left **A set of weighing scales accurate to 0.01g is essential for measuring out small quantities of starter culture.**

below right **A strainer and cheesecloth can be used for draining curds.**

a set of suitable lidded buckets of this capacity would be a wise investment since they are suitable for coagulation as well as for collecting whey or brining cheeses.

Pans and double-boilers Some of the recipes for harder cheeses require one or more stainless-steel pans for scalding. At the most basic level, a pan on the hob over a low heat may suffice, but there is a chance that the milk will burn on the base of the pan. For more sophisticated experiments in cheesemaking, it is possible to set up a simple double-boiler that emulates a water-jacketed cheese vat found in professional dairies. To do this, you will need two pans, one of which fits inside the other. Partially fill the larger pan with water; you need to add just enough to ensure that when the smaller pan is positioned inside the larger the water level comes to just below the tops of the pans. Fill the smaller pan with milk and place the double-boiler on the hob. With this arrangement, the temperature of the milk pan can continue to rise a few degrees after the hob is turned off due to retained heat in the surrounding water. With a bit of trial and error, you should be able to establish what temperature the milk should be when you turn off the heat in order for it to subsequently carry on heating up to the target temperature. This helps the cheesemaker avoid overshooting the target temperature and is a more gentle and controlled method of heating milk to a specific temperature.

Draining table The weekend cheesemaker may be happy enough to use a normal sink draining board, but for the more ambitious or regular cheesemaker it may be beneficial to buy or create a draining table. Buying a specialist one can be quite expensive, and you can easily create your own from many types of new or second-hand stainless-steel catering table. To do so, simply unscrew the top of the table and flip it over, neatly drill out a drainage hole in the middle of one end of the tabletop and, voilà, you have a ready-made draining table at a fraction of the price of a custom-made one. A third option is to use food-grade stacking crates that will accommodate all of your moulds, and simply drill a drainage hole in one corner. This has two advantages: crate sides help to stop the moulds falling over during turning, and they can easily be moved out of the way when family life begins to impinge on the dairy space.

opposite left **Strong, lidded food-grade buckets and containers are ideal for cheesemaking.**

opposite middle **You can create your own double-boiler from two pans.**

opposite right **Standard colanders can be used for draining curds, so long as they are adequately cleaned.**

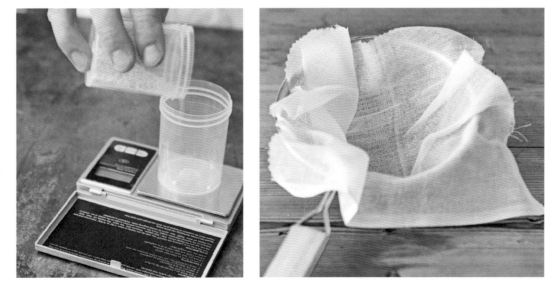

left **The temperature at which cheeses are matured and subsequently stored is important. Different types of cheese require different temperatures and storage methods during the maturation process, including a cool room, though once ready most types can then be kept in a standard domestic refrigerator to prevent them from spoiling.**

Drainage mats Some drainage mats made out of plastic mesh may be useful when salting or maturing cheese, or when draining soft cheeses in cylindrical moulds. Whey and condensation do not drain particularly well from very fine mesh, which also tends to be quite flimsy, so the most useful grades of mesh will be in the region of 1.5–5mm/0.06–0.2in. A couple of metres/yards of each should suffice.

Moulds Numerous moulds of varying shapes and sizes are available to buy, but much cheaper alternatives and instructions on how to make your own simple cheese moulds are covered on pages 18–19.

Curd-draining bag The Fresh Curd recipe on pages 82–5 calls for a curd-draining bag, which can be readily obtained from a cheesemaking supplies' store. Alternatively, a clean, sterilized pillowcase makes a good substitute. This kind of compromise in the quality of equipment does not have to translate into a lack of quality in the cheese; it is possible for a great cheesemaker to make good cheese using any clean, suitable equipment and for an unskilled cheesemaker to produce terrible cheeses using the best and most expensive equipment.

Cheesecloths While it is possible to cut drainage cloths from a large cotton or muslin sheet, you can also buy disposable cheesecloths for draining curd. The latter (often blue in colour) are intended for single use, but the home cheesemaker may be able to wash them a few times and reuse them before they deteriorate significantly. In addition to cheesecloth for draining, about 1m/1yd of muslin (usually white) will be required for larding and cloth-binding cheeses such as Cheddar. NB, while it is possible to wash cheesecloths used for draining, it is best to use new cloth for cloth-binding cheeses. Anyway, since the wrapping cloths will be thick with lard and moulds once the cheese is matured, it would simply not be possible to wash and reuse these afterwards.

Thermometer You will need a digital thermometer accurate to 0.1 of a degree. A waterproof thermometer, such as the dishwasher-safe models, can be a sensible option; it is likely to take a plunge into the milk or whey eventually…

pH meter It is possible to buy a relatively cheap pH meter, which will suit the purposes of the home cheesemaker. It should be accurate to ±0.01 of a pH point (see pages 36–7). pH papers are sometimes recommended to home cheesemakers, but with an accuracy of about ±0.2 to ±0.5 of a pH point, they will not deliver meaningful results and will make it hard to produce consistently good cheese. Cow's milk yields only about 1kg/2¼lb of cheese for every 10 litres/2.6 US gallons of milk, and sheep's milk a little more; it would be a pity to waste good milk making indifferent cheese for the want of a pH meter.

Weighing and measuring devices The small quantities of rennet required by the recipes may best be measured using a small measuring tube or syringe, while a small set of weighing scales accurate to 0.01g would be useful for measuring the starter. A calculator is extremely helpful when working out how much starter to use, and some screw-top plastic containers are useful for storing the starters after the packets have been opened. Don't forget to label the containers.

Utensils Many of the other pieces of equipment required for the home dairy are readily available in the kitchen, such as ladles, knives, slotted spoons, colanders, strainers, teaspoons and measuring jugs or cups. A balloon whisk with fine wires makes an acceptable alternative to a curd-knife, bearing a superficial resemblance to the *spino* that is used to cut the curds during the production of Parmigiano. A few recipes, including the one for Cheddar, may call for a curd mill to chop up the acidified curds prior to salting. However, this is a specialized piece of equipment that may be of limited use, in which case chopping up the curd with a knife or shredding it manually would probably make more sense. A yogurt-maker can be a useful piece of equipment but, for occasional makes, a wide-necked vacuum flask with a 500ml/17fl oz-capacity makes an acceptable substitute.

Maturing racks Wire cake-cooling racks bear some resemblance to the metal racks used for the maturation of soft cheeses, but the quality of the metal can be poor and may start to rust quickly given the combination of salt, moisture and acidity on the surface of cheese. A better, and cheap, option may be to place cheeses on a plastic board lined with some plastic mesh.

REFRIGERATION

Rennet needs to be stored in a standard refrigerator, and starter cultures in the freezer, but some careful consideration needs to be given to refrigeration when it comes to the maturation of cheeses; the domestic refrigerator can be used to store some of the fresh and brined ones in this book, but it may not make the best maturation environment for some of the ripened ones.

The occasional cheesemaker may be able to place cheeses in a domestic refrigerator in a lidded plastic food container lined with plastic mesh so long as they drain off any condensation each day and wash the container regularly to prevent the growth of *Pseudomonas*. Home cheesemakers interested in surface-ripened soft cheese or blue cheese and who are planning more than the odd batch, however, would do well to acquire a second-hand wine fridge, which operates at the optimum temperatures required for cheese maturation. Alternatively, with a little engineering, a standard domestic refrigerator can be modified for cheese maturation by wiring it into a thermostatic controller, such as the kind used to regulate the temperature of an aquarium. The optimum temperature for maturing most types of cheese falls in the region of 10–15°C/50–59°F, with a temperature of 12°C/54°F being a good target. However, once fully ripened, soft cheeses need to be wrapped and transferred to a colder refrigerator to hold back any further development, and a standard domestic refrigerator is suitable for this purpose. Whatever you choose to do, a digital refrigerator thermometer is useful for monitoring the temperature of your 'cheese store'.

Hard cheeses, on the other hand, may not require refrigerated storage at all; maturation on wooden boards in a cool place at 10–15°C/50–59°F may be a better alternative. I have reviewed the available scientific literature on the safety of wood as a food contact surface in the dairy and found that, as long as it is completely clean and in good condition, wood is no worse than many of the alternatives. It is worth noting, however, that while wood has many positive attributes for the maturation of semi-hard and hard cheeses, it may pose a hygiene risk when used with soft cheeses and therefore should be avoided.

As a guide to how long dairy products can be safely stored, 'use by' times have been supplied in recipes for products that become less safe over time. Hard cheeses, however, will become more safe and there isn't really an upper age limit – they will just become harder and drier but remain good to eat.

WOODEN EQUIPMENT

The use of wood as a food contact material is considered traditional in many cheese-producing countries. In France, however, the use of wood was enshrined in law in the *Arrêté du 15 Novembre 1945*, which permitted cheesemakers to use: oak, hornbeam, sweet chestnut, ash, false acacia, walnut, beech, elm and poplar for food contact. In 2006, silver fir, Norway spruce, Douglas fir, maritime pine, Scots pine, beech, plane, aspen, alder, olive and birch were added to the list.

In some regions, wood is not only used for the maturation of cheese but also for cheesemaking itself – notable examples being wooden vats, such as the *gerles* used in the production of Salers in the Auvergne, and the *tina* used to make Ragusano, a stretched-curd cheese from Sicily.

Cheese Moulds

With the exception of bag-drained curds, many of the cheese recipes described in this book will require moulds, also sometimes referred to as 'hoops' or 'forms'. There is an almost bewildering array of shapes and sizes available and some will be suitable for more than one cheese type. The shape and appearance of the mould will give a lot of information about the kind of curd it is designed to hold.

SOFT-CHEESE MOULDS

Soft- and lactic-cheese moulds are generally greater in height than they are in diameter. Soft-cheese curds usually shrink down by up to two-thirds during drainage and these moulds are not normally lined with cheesecloth so they are commonly sold with ample drainage holes on the base and sides.

Some of these moulds are beaker-shaped while others may be open-ended cylinders. The latter type requires some plastic drainage mesh. Soft cheeses are not pressed, so their moulds generally do not have lids, or 'followers'. The moulds are usually round but occasionally square shapes are available – usually used for Pont l'Évêque and similar soft cheeses.

Some lactic-cheese moulds may be of narrow diameter, often smaller than a Camembert, with a height that is shorter than the diameter. Allowing for the fact that it will drain down to one-third of the initial height, cheese made in this mould would be little taller than a biscuit or cookie – a telltale sign that the moulds are intended to be used for shaping pre-drained lactic curds. They are available in a variety of shapes, including hearts and pyramids.

You may see references to 'multi-moulds', which are large moulds that will form around a dozen soft cheeses at a time. Due to the volume of milk required they are not really suitable for the home cheesemaker and are intended for use in more industrial approaches to cheesemaking.

SEMI-HARD-CHEESE MOULDS

Cheeses such as Reblochon, which fall somewhere between soft and semi-hard, resemble to some extent the soft-cheese moulds but they are shorter and the drainage holes may be fewer in number. Soft, wet curds draining to one-third of their initial height would produce a cheese something akin to a pancake in one of these moulds, which tells us that these they are intended for curd that is finely cut and well-stirred and that is expected to drain only by about a half rather than two-thirds. These moulds may be lined with cheesecloth and drainage may be aided by placing a small weight on top of the cheese for a limited period of time.

HOW TO MAKE A CHEESE MOULD

Plastic buckets and containers can easily be turned into cheese moulds suitable for use by the home cheesemaker. When drilling plastic, it helps to have a cold drill bit to avoid 'burring' of the plastic, so put the drill bit in the freezer for a few minutes before using it. Heat will build up in the bit as you drill, so return it to the freezer briefly if it becomes overheated. Avoid hard, brittle plastics since these tend to crack, and do not put too much pressure on the plastic. Let the drill do the hard work.

For a hard-cheese mould, take two small plastic buckets of approximately the same size. One will be the mould while the other will be the follower and this should fit snugly into the mould. Drill a series of drainage holes in the base of the mould using a 5mm/¼in drill bit. To use the mould, line it with with cheesecloth. The 'lid' may be filled with weights to press the cheese.

For a soft-cheese mould suitable for Brie-type cheeses, only one bucket is needed. Cut a circular hole in the middle of the base of the bucket, leaving a small lip around the edge. Cut a disc of plastic mesh to fit inside the bucket, resting on the base. A moulding plate, of the type used to shape bag-drained lactic curds for Rocamadour production, can easily be made by drilling out holes from a 15mm/¾in-thick polypropylene chopping board using a 6cm/2½in hole saw.

HARD-CHEESE MOULDS

These moulds are generally wider than they are tall. The drainage holes are often few in number and sometimes located only on the base, indicating that these moulds should be used with a cheesecloth. The sides of the mould will be smooth and the moulds will usually have a follower that fits inside to help the cheesemaker to squeeze out whey during pressing. A variation of this type of mould, sometimes seen in Gouda production, is a plastic mould and follower with a reusable plastic net that takes the place of cheesecloth.

Cheddar moulds are very often made of stainless steel but, for home production, a 1–2kg/2¼–4½lb-capacity plastic mould may be suitable for the harder cheeses.

Micro-perforated cheese moulds and followers have tiny drainage holes, almost invisible to the eye, and the inside of the mould is textured. These moulds do not require a cheesecloth. The drainage holes can easily become blocked, so they must be cleaned in hot water with nitric or phosphoric acid (caustic products can cause the cheeses to stick in the moulds). They are not suitable for soft cheeses as they do not drain well without being pressed.

DIY MOULDS

The home cheesemaker doesn't need to spend a fortune on moulds. Professionals have found many inventive ways of making them over the years, including adapting plastic piping, containers, buckets and, more unusually, the baskets typically used for pond plants. Colanders can also be used to produce soft blue cheeses as well as hard and semi-hard cheeses.

If you choose to make them yourself, in order to avoid concerns over migration of plastics into your cheese, it is best only to use materials sold as being for 'food use'.

opposite left **Moulds are available in a wide range of shapes and sizes and with varying numbers and gauges of drainage holes depending on the type of cheese that will be made.**

opposite right **Some moulds are lined with cheesecloth, which may be blue.**

left **You can adapt everyday items for home cheesemaking.**

Food Safety and Hygiene

There are a number of bacteria in dairy products that can cause food poisoning, and awareness of the risks can help the home cheesemaker to control them. I'm not going to go into the clinical behaviour of each pathogen in any great depth nor discuss how they can be controlled at milk-production level as the home cheesemaker is not likely to have control of this, but there are some key hygiene and food-safety procedures that should always be followed when making cheese.

The number of reported cases of *Salmonella* and *Listeria monocytogenes* in relation to cheese is really fairly low. To mitigate the slim chances of food contamination, professional food-manufacturing plants adhere to very strict guidelines and processes, but these may be rather over-the-top for the home cheesemaker. In general, a little common sense and awareness goes a long way when it comes to controlling many of the food-safety risks you will encounter.

HYGIENE GUIDELINES

• Wash your hands before making cheese, after blowing your nose and after going to the toilet. It sounds obvious, but it is incredibly important that hands are properly cleaned when you are making cheese. Try to be aware of what you are doing with your hands and wash them again after touching your face or emptying the bin or trash can. For proper, effective hand-washing technique, see the box opposite.

• *Staphylococcus aureus* is found as part of the normal microflora on the skin and in the nose of many people (in fact most of us carry it at one point or another during our lives). With good hand hygiene and by keeping any damaged skin covered, however, it is unlikely to cause a problem when making cheese, but do cover cuts, lesions and damaged skin with a waterproof sticking plaster and avoid making cheese when suffering from skin, eye and ear infections.

left **Stringent procedures are employed by commercial cheese manufacturers and in stores that sell cheese, with food safety being a primary concern. Although some of the measures are a little extreme for the occasional home cheesemaker, the same basic hygiene guidelines apply, especially with regard to hand-washing and general cleanliness during the make itself and while storing and handling the cheese.**

• Vomiting and diarrhoea, abdominal pain or fever are common symptoms of food-poisoning infections including *Salmonella*, *Listeria monocytogenes*, Shiga toxin-producing *E.coli* (STEC) such as *E.coli* O157, and *Campylobacter*. Avoid making cheese when symptomatic and for at least 48 hours after recovery.

• Few home cheesemakers have their own small dairy, so there are a number of considerations when making cheese in a shared space such as a kitchen. These include cleaning equipment and work surfaces (see pages 22–3); and keeping all pets – including birds, reptiles and amphibians, which can carry *Salmonella* – out of the cheesemaking area.

• Keep buckets and containers containing milk and curd covered to exclude flying insects and dust.

• Due to the risks of cross-contamination, do not handle raw meat or its packaging, or eggs in their shells, in the same area and at the same time as making cheese.

• The five-second rule does not apply to cheesemaking (or, indeed to anything; it is a myth!). If a piece of equipment lands on the floor, it should be washed and disinfected before use. You should also wash your hands after touching anything that has been in contact with the floor, which can harbour *Listeria monocytogenes* and many other harmful organisms.

KNOW THE DANGERS

Many food-poisoning bacteria can cause severe complications, or death, with the elderly, young children, pregnant women and the immunocompromised considered to be at greatest risk. The principal means by which these bacteria can be controlled by a home cheesemaker is pasteurization of the milk and good hygienic practice during the production of the cheese.

High-risk foods include raw milk and unpasteurized dairy products, and raw and pasteurized soft and mould-ripened cheeses. These pose a particular risk of *L. monocytogenes*, which can grow during refrigerated storage. This may be less common than other food-poisoning bacteria, but pregnant women are more susceptible to infection and this can result in miscarriage.

In addition to generally being at increased risk from most food-poisoning bacteria, children seem to be particularly at risk of severe complications following STEC infection – including kidney failure and death.

HOW TO WASH YOUR HANDS

Good hand-washing technique is one of the principal methods of infection control if done effectively. Use liquid soap and hot water and wash your hands for at least 30 seconds, scrubbing your palms with your nails, interlacing and rubbing the fingers, remembering to clean the thumb rotationally and to clean the wrists and forearms. If your nails are dirty, use a brush and soap to scrub them clean. Rinse and dry your hands afterwards. Disposable towels would be preferable but, at the very least, hands should be dried on a clean towel. Alcohol hand gels and plastic gloves are no substitute for proper hand washing. Antibacterial soap can be used, but remember that without good hand-washing technique it may be less effective than ordinary soap that has been applied correctly.

Staphylococcus aureus is a minor pathogen that can produce a heat-stable enterotoxin that causes rapid but ultimately short-lived vomiting and diarrhoea. High levels of *S. aureus* are required to produce the toxin, which remains in the food even after the bacteria have died. This bacteria is a weak competitor in comparison to the starter LAB and tends to die during cheese-ripening. Batches of cheese in which acidification fails or is stalled should be considered to pose a risk of *Staphylococcal* growth and enterotoxin production, as should cheese made from raw milk from mastitic animals; *S. aureus* is a common cause of mastitis in milking herds.

Several other species of *Staphylococcus* are harmless ripening organisms (see Mould-ripening and Rind-washing on pages 42–5 for more details).

Cleaning and Disinfection

The amount of cleaning that is involved during cheesemaking can surprise some people, but as we have seen, dairy products can make a good source of food for some undesirable bacteria so it is especially important that cheesemaking equipment is cleaned effectively.

Thoroughly cleaning and disinfecting a cheesemaking area or kitchen is a two-stage process. The first is cleaning, which involves the application of hot water, some detergent and mechanical action (such as scrubbing) to physically remove dirt from the surface of the equipment, before it is rinsed in clean water. The second is disinfection, which treats equipment to kill

the (hopefully) small number of microbes that might have survived the cleaning process. This is carried out using some disinfectant diluted in cold water at a specified dose and for a specified time, before the equipment is rinsed in clean water.

Disinfection without prior cleaning is ineffective, since surface dirt reduces the activity of the disinfectant and allows large numbers of bacteria to survive in deposits of grease and protein. Cleaning, even if it is very effective, cannot remove all of the bacteria from a surface: in short, the two must go hand-in-hand. Check equipment after it has been washed; if it is greasy then it has not been cleaned effectively and should be cleaned again before being disinfected.

Assuming that you will be making cheese infrequently, the best practice is to clean dirty equipment immediately after using it, rinse it and allow it to dry before storing it. When you come to use it again, clean it once more and rinse it before disinfecting it, observing the correct contact time and dilution and then rinsing the equipment thoroughly once more in clean water. Rinsing off the disinfectant is important, because traces left on cheesemaking equipment can inhibit the starter bacteria and leave undesirable flavour taints in the cheese.

CLEANING EQUIPMENT

• The home cheesemaker can make use of two or possibly three household chemicals. Washing-up detergent is cheap and readily available. It is perhaps not as heavy duty as something like chlorinated caustic powder, but it should prove adequate for the home cheesemaker. Look for one with anionic surfactant content over 15 per cent. Some of the cheaper detergents fall short of this and are less good at degreasing equipment. The typical dose of detergent may be around 5ml/1 tsp per 1 litre/34fl oz hot water at 50–60°C/122–140°F, in which solution the equipment should be scrubbed manually before then being thoroughly rinsed in cold water. Alternatively, you can wash cheesemaking equipment in the dishwasher.

left **Spotlessly clean and disinfected equipment should be neatly stored in a safe place so that it is accessible yet kept away from potential contaminants. At home, try to set aside a shelf dedicated to cheesemaking equipment so that it stays clean and tidy.**

• For disinfection, sodium hypochlorite (bleach) or sterilizing tablets are cheap, effective and widely available. A bleach containing 10 per cent hypochlorite should be diluted to 2.5ml/ ½ tsp per 1 litre/34fl oz cold water and equipment should be soaked for a 2-minute contact time. NB, whatever product you use, refer to the manufacturer's instructions. Chlorine-based disinfectants can leave flavour taints so make sure you rinse equipment thoroughly and be careful not to mix hypochlorite with acid-based products as the reaction will release toxic chlorine gas.

• In hard-water areas, it may also be necessary to use an acid product, such as hydrochloric acid, to remove 'milkstone', a white scaly deposit, from cheese moulds. This should be readily available at a hardware store but, for a limited number of moulds, a cupful of vinegar may suffice.

• A plastic scrubbing brush designated for cheesemaking equipment may be a good idea. Clean and disinfect it regularly – this can be done in the dishwasher. Household sponges and dishcloths, on the other hand, are an excellent source of undesirable bacteria and should be avoided.

• Work surfaces should also be cleaned before being used for cheesemaking. To do so, first wash them with hot, soapy water then wipe them down with some disinfectant solution. Use a sponge or cloth designated solely for this purpose and sterilize it frequently by putting it in the top rack of the dishwasher and running a hot cycle.

• The best way to clean reusable cheesecloths and curd-draining bags is to rinse off the curd residue and then wash them in hot soapy water. After washing, rinse them well and boil them in hot water for a few minutes before hanging them out to dry.

• If you don't have a curd-draining bag and want to make fresh cheese, you can use a cotton pillowcase or small sheet instead, if you clean it properly. To do this, tie togther the four corners of the sheet, if using, and place it or the pillowcase in a large pan of boiling water. Boil it for about 10 minutes to thoroughly sterilize it and remove any traces of washing detergent.

left **Kitchen cloths can harbour bacteria so use a new, washed and disinfected cloth for cheesemaking when one is needed or use a scrubbing brush instead.**

above **Cheesemaking equipment must always be carefully cleaned and disinfected before use – whether at home or in a commerical cheese-manufacturing factory.**

Sourcing Milk

Sourcing milk can be one of biggest problems in cheesemaking, unless you are fortunate enough to have your own milking animals or there is a nearby farm that is able to supply milk. In farmhouse cheesemaking, all aspects of milk production may be controlled to produce a raw material that has been optimized specifically for the cheese being made. The home cheesemaker can't have this level of control and must make a concession regarding milk quality without compromising on safety.

To avoid the inference of any bias in the following comments, I would like to make it clear that I have commercial experience of making both pasteurized and raw-milk cheese. That the raw-milk cheeses were soft cheeses matured for around 30–60 days shows that this can be done safely with the right process controls in place. As someone who also advises businesses on issues of food safety, however, I must give a balanced view of the risks.

RAW OR UNPASTEURIZED MILK?

This is milk that has not been heated above 40°C/104°F. It has many highly vocal advocates but it is not without its risks and these can be difficult to quantify for the home cheesemaker. Unpasteurized milk that is heat-treated to about 63°C/145°F for 15 seconds prior to cheesemaking is described as 'thermized milk'. This is usually done to control spoilage organisms such as *Pseudomonas* and *coliforms* but will not control many of the more serious pathogens.

Not having undergone heat-treatment, raw milk can show excellent coagulation properties but it would be irresponsible not to consider the possible presence of pathogens including: *Mycobacterium bovis* (bovine TB); *Brucella*; Shiga toxin-producing *Escherichia coli*; *Listeria monocytogenes*; *Staphylococcus aureus*; *Campylobacter*; *Bacillus cereus*; and *Salmonella*. This list is by no

left **Milk from Jersey cows is especially rich and creamy, although this in itself is no guarantee of an improvement in the quality of the cheese it can be used to make.**

right **Whether raw or pasteurized, milk should be used as fresh as possible, and stored at the correct temperature in the refrigerator.**

means exhaustive. These pathogens may be present but not detectable, either because they are there in insufficient quantities to be detected or because they are missed during sampling.

Raw milk needs to come from a herd that is free from TB and Brucellosis. Do not try to obtain raw milk where the farm is not permitted to sell it or local law prohibits it. Milk that is intended to be drunk raw should be subject to more stringent monitoring of microbiological quality than milk intended for pasteurization, for which plate counts and somatic cell counts are principally used to assess hygienic quality. These tests are not reliable indicators of the presence of pathogens in raw milk. Bacteria such as *Listeria monocytogenes* and the spoilage organism *Pseudomonas* can grow during cold storage, so the milk should be less than 12–24 hours old and stored below 4°C/39°F.

All of this considered, even milk that passes the criteria for sale as raw drinking milk may still not be of a suitable standard for cheesemaking; pathogens can grow during production or ripening of cheese and home cheesemakers rarely, if ever, carry out routine microbiological analysis. Raw milk is therefore not without its dangers, but there are a couple of ways that determined raw-milk cheesemakers can perhaps reduce their risk:

• Buy raw milk from a farm that is permitted to sell it and that also makes raw-milk cheese – especially soft cheese.
• Follow a hard-cheese recipe with a relatively fast acidification, high scald temperature and longer ripening time – such as Grana Padano or Parmesan cheese.

This does not, however, constitute an endorsement of the safety of the use of raw milk in home cheesemaking.

RAW MILK AND IMMUNITY

Sometimes it seems that everyone knows of someone who 'drank raw milk on the farm every day from childhood and lived to the age of 102', but it might be worth considering that a person who did not grow up on that farm drinking raw milk since childhood cannot expect to have the same level of natural immunity. It is advisable to tread cautiously if you are new to drinking raw milk – especially in the case of children.

Anyone with a vague understanding of workings of the immune system would probably agree that there may be some truth in the claim that raw milk can boost the immune system, but in order to develop immunity to a pathogen a person needs to have been exposed to it. If raw milk is 'free from pathogens' then it cannot help to confer adaptive immunity. Several studies seem to suggest that *Listeria monocytogenes* is present in around 5–6 per cent of raw milk samples, mostly at low levels.

Raw drinking milk enjoyed on the farm is also likely to be very fresh. During the first 2 hours after milking, milk receives optimal protection from naturally occurring anti-microbial compounds and enzymes such as Lactoperoxidase. The level of protection decreases with time, especially if due diligence isn't given to temperature control. Bear in mind that domestic refrigerators are rarely as cold as their owners think they are.

PASTEURIZED MILK

This is milk that has been heated to 72°C/161°F for 15 seconds or, less commonly, to 63°C/145°F for 30 minutes. The heat treatment reduces pathogens to harmless levels and kills many of the common spoilage organisms but it may also impair coagulation properties, especially where the pasteurization temperature or time are increased to extend the milk's shelf-life.

Growth of *Pseudomonas* prior to pasteurization can leave heat-stable enzymes that can continue to damage the milk. The oxidized flavours characteristic of this kind of enzymatic degradation are, unfortunately, becoming all too common in bottled milk. The words 'fresh milk' on the supermarket product can mean very little – some of the milk will already have been 2 days old when it was collected from the farm.

below left **Milk sold at supermarkets is sometimes a few days old even before it hits the shelves, so it may be worth locating a fresher source.**

right **Milk intended for commercially-produced cheese is carefully selected and monitored. For the home cheesemaker, freshness is the best guide.**

Pasteurized milk is not sterile; spore-forming bacteria such as *Clostridium tyrobutyricum* may survive the pasteurization process and contribute to gas defects in some cheese varieties. I have seen some spectacular examples of late-blowing defect in cheeses made from supermarket milk. Other spoilage bacteria, including *Pseudomonas*, may be killed by pasteurization but reintroduced by low-level contamination on the bottling line. Some dairies seem to be worse than others in this regard.

Contrary to popular belief, these things considered, there is no guaranteed improvement in the cheesemaking potential of pasteurized whole organic milk, unhomogenized milk or milk from Jersey or Guernsey cows, over standard homogenized whole milk. The same is true of adding cream to the milk. Freshness and pasteurization are the primary concerns for cheesemakers.

Where milk is marketed not on freshness but on price, small dairy processors tend to get squeezed out of the market but, with increasing interest in local food-production, I hope that on-farm processing will become more common. If you can find a farmer who has diversified into pasteurizing and bottling milk, ideally on the day of production, then this could be a good way to balance food safety and spoilage considerations. The farmer can also prove to be a valuable source of information about their herd, including details such as their average lactation stage and milk composition.

While it may be easier to get hold of cow's milk, some of the recipes in this book are well suited to sheep's or goat's milk while others may be adapted to suit them – principally by modifying the coagulation time (see pages 34–5).

PSEUDOMONAS

Because of their ability to grow at temperatures as cold as 4°C/39°F, 'psychrotrophic' (cold-tolerant) bacteria such as *Pseudomonas* are some of the principal spoilage bacteria in many foods, including milk and dairy products.

Pseudomonas species are ubiquitous and, possessing no complex nutritional requirements, they are able to grow quickly in wet environments, producing biofilms to confer increased resistance to disinfection. They are even able to use soap residues as a food source! They secrete powerful proteolytic enzymes that can damage casein, producing bitter peptides, as well as lipolytic enzymes that can cause rancidity. These enzymes are more heat-stable than the bacteria that produce them and remain active after pasteurization. Even if you intend to pasteurize raw milk before using it for cheesemaking, this fact makes a strong case for using the milk while it is very fresh.

Pseudomonas fluorescens, one of the most common species involved in dairy spoilage, produces a yellow-green pigment, pyoverdine, which is fluorescent under ultra-violet light and is sometimes found on the rinds of surface-ripened cheeses – particularly washed-rind ones. Their presence is best avoided through scrupulous hygienic practice (see Cleaning and Disinfection on pages 22–3).

Starter Cultures

In cheesemaking, starter cultures are the key to making a safe cheese. These contain a mixture of lactic acid bacteria (LAB) that are added to milk to enable a controlled and consistent acidification that will hinder the growth of less acid-tolerant and less-desirable bacteria such as *Listeria*. LAB convert lactose, the sugar present in milk, into lactic acid, which reduces the pH of the cheese and in doing so removes a food source that could be utilized by any bad bacteria that may be present in the milk.

We will be adding starter cultures to almost all of the recipes for making cheese in this book. Some cheeses, such as the Paneer on pages 70–3, are made not by using starters but by direct acidification; the pH drop required for coagulation being achieved by the addition of a quantity of lactic or citric acid. Since no bacteria have been added to the milk, the lactose is not fermented into lactic acid so it remains in the curd as a food source for bacterial growth. It would be unwise to attempt to

left **Different types of cheese require starter cultures suited to the conditions of production, such as the thermophilic (heat-tolerant) cultures used to make this Gruyère.**

use the direct acidification method for anything other than a fresh, low-pH cheese, the acidity and short shelf-life of which control many of the food-safety risks.

Left in a warm place, it is possible for the low levels of naturally occurring LAB present in raw milk to acidify spontaneously. It is, however, also possible for less-desirable bacteria to grow in the same conditions. In pasteurized milk, most of the natural LAB will have been killed off along with any pathogenic bacteria by the heat-treatment. The use of starter cultures is therefore a necessity. In short, it is good practice to add starter cultures to milk if you want to make cheese safely and consistently.

Starter cultures are highly specialized products that you will need to buy in, along with rennet, from a specialist retailer. There is a number of online businesses that can supply small quantities of these products to the home cheesemaker.

By and large, the cultures you are most likely to encounter on these websites will have been produced either by Christian Hansen or Danisco, so I have specified which of their respective cultures to use in each recipe. This does not mean that you cannot substitute a different culture from an alternative manufacturer, however, so I've also included a description of the type of starter used so you can easily and correctly substitute an alternative product.

TYPES OF STARTER CULTURE

Direct Vat Inoculation (DVI) starters, which are the type that the home cheesemaker is most likely to use, are freeze-dried cultures intended to be added directly to the milk and stirred in. Liquid starter cultures and whey starters are less suitable for the home cheesemaker, though we will explore a version of bulk starter later in the book (see Cheddar Cheese on pages 116–23).

DVI starters contain living products and they are packaged not by volume but by activity, expressed here either in Units (U) or Danisco Culture Units (DCU). To measure out the quantity of starter required, you will need a small set of scales that can read down to 0.01g. It is possible (but not advisable) to open the pack and divide it up by sight, but this will result in inconsistency from one make to the next. Cheesemaking can be a wildly variable process anyway without the cheesemaker introducing more problems, so it is worth investing in suitable weighing scales.

HOW TO CALCULATE THE WEIGHT OF STARTER TO USE

Use this simple equation to calculate how much starter is required for a recipe:

Weight of starter required (g) = Units required (U) × Weight of starter in whole sachet (g) ÷ Units in whole sachet (U)

Q: A recipe calls for 2 units of starter culture. The sachet contains 50U and weighs 10.2g. How much starter should be weighed out?

A: Weight of starter required (g) = 2U × 10.2g ÷ 50U = 0.408g
The scales are accurate to 0.01g so this would be rounded up to 0.41g.

left **The flavour of hard ripened cheeses such as this Wrekin White depends in part on strains of LAB present in the starter culture and the enzymes they release during ripening.**

Some suppliers will package smaller sachets of starters and occasionally a starter may be packaged according to the volume of milk it can inoculate. The step-by-step instructions are intended for larger sachets sold by the unit but they can be adapted for other starters. DVI cultures should be stored in the freezer. It is possible to use them beyond their durability date, though activity may decline with time.

Starter cultures are often described as being thermophilic or mesophilic. The type of cheese you are making will determine which type of starter you need. Thermophiles are bacteria that like heat: they will not grow below 30°C/86°F. Their heat tolerance means that they grow well in cheeses with a high scald temperature, such as Parmigiano Reggiano, which is heated to 55°C/131°F during the make.

Mesophiles, however, prefer 'medium' temperatures, neither too hot nor too cold, and they constitute a large number of the LAB we will encounter as well as many of the pathogens we wish to avoid. Mesophiles grow best in the temperature range between 20–40°C/68–104°F, meaning that they are ideal for making, say, a lactic cheese that is coagulated at 21°C/70°F, a temperature at which a thermophile would not grow or acidify. By contrast, mesophiles would not be able to grow at the high temperature used during the Parmigiano Reggiano make, so would not be suitable for that cheese.

Mesophiles are often also described as either being heterofermentative or homofermentative: heterofermentative LAB produce lactic acid as well as a range of aroma compounds and exhibit some gas production that can help to create small holes in the cheese paste. These starters are also sometimes called 'aromatic' starter cultures. Homofermentative LAB only produce lactic acid, without the gas production or aroma compounds, and they tend to acidify faster. Perhaps slightly confusingly, most starters described as being 'heterofermentative cultures' will actually be made up of a significant proportion of homofermentative LAB species to help with the acidification.

With so many cultures available, people are often surprised to find out that many different cheese varieties can be made with only a few different starters, so a few sachets can go a long way. Some of the different species of LAB, the starter cultures they are found in, and their practical applications are outlined in the table opposite.

In addition to LAB, starter cultures for ripened cheeses are sometimes blended with other bacteria or fungi (yeasts or moulds) or these may be available as a separate culture. These microbes will not contribute to the acidification and the achievement of a 'safe' pH but will help with the breakdown of the cheese and subsequent flavour development, so they are more properly described as being 'ripening cultures' (see Mould-ripening and Rind-washing on pages 42–5).

Don't worry too much about the species names of the various LAB; it is possible to make good cheese without a degree in microbiology. I've included them in the table that follows and in recipes as they often appear in product descriptions or specifications. The list of products is by no means exhaustive and the table may be helpful when trying to decipher a cheesemaking supplies' catalogue.

Flora Danica, CHN-11 and CHN-19 or MM-100 and MM-10 are examples of 'rotation starters', which means that one can be substituted for the other. Commercial dairies will rotate starter types to avoid issues with bacteriophage, which can stall the acidification (see Troubleshooting on pages 198–9). However, it should not be essential for a home cheesemaker to rotate their starters due to the occasional and limited nature of their production.

HOW TO MEASURE OUT STARTER CULTURES

1 Tare (zero) some weighing scales that can read down to 0.01g using a clean, dry plastic container.

2 Open the starter sachet, then pour out and weigh the entire contents of the sachet. Record this weight.

3 Calculate the weight required using the equation on page 29 and tare the weight of another container.

4 Weigh out the amount of starter needed and add it to the milk as outlined in the recipe.

5 Return the unused starter IMMEDIATELY to the freezer, marking the container clearly with the name of the starter and the weight of the full pack so that you can accurately calculate the units and weight of starter required for any subsequent recipes.

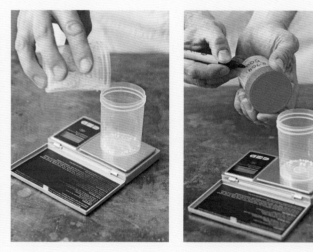

TABLE OF STARTER CULTURES

Species of lactic acid bacteria		Examples of cultures	Examples of cheese types made with these cultures
MESOPHILES – Grow at 20–40°C/68–104°F			
Homofermentative Produce lactic acid only	*Lactococcus lactis* subsp. *lactis* *Lactococcus lactis* subsp. *cremoris*	R-703, R-704, MA-11, MA-14	fresh cheeses brined cheeses
Heterofermentative Produce lactic acid, gas and aroma compounds	*Lactococcus lactis* subsp. *lactis* biovar *diacetylactis* *Leuconostoc mesenteroides*	Cultures also include homofermentative strains: Flora Danica, CHN-11, CHN-19, Probat 222, Probat 322, MM-100, MM-101	Gouda Camembert Cheddar Cheshire Stilton
THERMOPHILES – Only grow at temperatures above 30°C/86°F			
	Streptococcus thermophilus	ST-M7, TA-50	mozzarella
		STB-01, STAM-3	Gorgonzola Taleggio
	Lactobacillus delbrueckii subsp. *bulgaricus*	LB-12 with S. *thermophilus*: MY 800,	Reblochon Saint Nectaire
	Lactobacillus helveticus	ALP-D	Gruyère Parmesan

Rennet and Coagulation

While it is possible to coagulate curd through acidification alone, it is more common to use rennet to speed up the whole process. Traditionally, an extract of the fourth stomach compartment of a calf, kid or lamb would have been used as a source of the rennet enzyme, chymosin, and it is still common to find animal rennet used in the production of cheese. That said, there is now a number of alternatives, outlined below.

DIFFERENT STRENGTHS OF RENNET

Beyond coagulation, rennet has a role in the proteolysis (see pages 12–13) and the ripening of cheese, though this is strongly dependent on the quantity of rennet retained in the curd. Just how much remains is influenced by the type of rennet used, the dose, and the pH of the curd at drainage.

Rennet strength can be expressed in International Milk Clotting Units (IMCU), Soxhlet Activity or as milligrams of chymosin. For example, a standard-strength rennet with an activity of 1:10,000 may have an IMCU of more than 140 and contain 500mg of chymosin. A reduced-strength rennet with an activity of 1:1000 may have an IMCU of 14 and contain 50mg of chymosin. The reduced-strength rennet is 1/10th of the strength of the standard rennet so 10 times as much is needed to clot the same volume of milk.

1:10,000 is the strength most commonly encountered in the UK, but it is also possible to get double- and triple-strength rennet more suitable for industrial-scale producers. In the USA, it can be more common to encounter rennet with an activity of 1:15,000. This is 1.5 times more concentrated than 1:10,000 rennet. Reduced-strength rennet is scarce but, where available, it is ideally suited to the needs of the home cheesemaker. Whichever type you use, store rennet in the refrigerator, returning the bottle immediately after use to avoid loss of activity.

The recipes in this book have been written giving strengths of 1:10,000 rennet, so scale the quantity as required to give the equivalent dose of stronger or weaker rennet.

left **Milking animals such as these goats yield not only milk but also the enzyme that can coagulate it – extracted from the fourth stomach compartment of kids, lambs and calves.**

right **Rennet is sold in various forms; this dried calf stomach (also known as vell or abomasum) is used in the production of some traditional cheeses.**

DIFFERENT TYPES OF RENNET

There is a number of different rennet types available to the home cheesemaker, available from cheesemaking suppliers:

Calf rennet An extract of the fourth stomach compartment of a calf, kid or lamb. E.g. Naturen.

Microbial rennet A protease enzyme extracted from fungi, usually a species of the mould *Rhizomucor*. The rennet coagulates milk by the same mechanism as animal rennet but is suitable for vegetarians. E.g. Hannilase, Marzyme.

Recombinant rennet The enzyme responsible for chymosin production in the animal is expressed in a vector organism to create large amounts of coagulant with the same properties as animal rennet but at a fraction of the cost. Recombinant rennet is suitable for vegetarians but is not permitted by organic-certification bodies. E.g. Chy-Max and Maxiren.

Vegetable rennet In Britain, Ladies Bedstraw (*Galium verum*) was used historically to coagulate milk when animal rennet was not available. Cardoon and fig sap coagulate milk in the same way. Vegetable coagulants are suitable for vegetarians but can be strongly proteolytic, producing characteristically bitter flavours.

Rennet paste Typically used for Provolone- and Pecorino-style cheeses, rennet pastes are prepared from the stomachs of milk-fed animals slaughtered after suckling. The stomachs are partially dried and turned into paste that is characterized by the presence of the lipase enzyme pre-gastric esterase. In the absence of the paste, it may be possible to substitute with rennet extract and lipase.

CARDOON-CHEESES OF THE IBERIAN PENINSULA

The stamen on the flower of the cardoon, or artichoke thistle, *(Cynara cardunculus)* is sometimes dried and used to prepare a rennet extract. It is traditionally employed in parts of Spain and Portugal to coagulate sheep's milk for cheeses such as Torta del Casar and Serra da Estrela.

These cheeses are quite strong-flavoured and can show a hint of bitterness on the finish. For this reason they are traditionally paired with a large piece of *membrillo* or quince paste, which provides a sweet counterpoint to the strong flavour of the cheese.

While cardoon rennet can be successfully used for making both sheep and goats' milk cheeses, be aware that it can produce unpalatably bitter results when used with cow's milk.

THE FLOCCULATION TEST

1 Fill a measuring cylinder with blood-warm water.

2 Dip a finger into the renneted milk and allow a drop to fall into the tube.

3 If the milk disperses, flocculation has not occurred.

4 If the milk forms solid flakes that sink towards the bottom of the tube, the flocculation point has been reached.

THE MECHANISM OF COAGULATION

Casein in the milk is organized in small units called micelles, from which hydrophilic (water-loving) kappa-casein tails protrude. The presence of these tails has a stabilizing effect on the structure of the micelle. The addition of rennet to milk cuts the end off the kappa-casein tail, destabilizing the micelles, which then begin to aggregate in the presence of calcium. The first stage of the process is called flocculation and is marked by the appearance of the initial signs of coagulation into a weak gel. You can test for this by performing the flocculation test outlined above.

During the second stage of coagulation, the gel becomes progressively harder through cross-linking of the micelles. The longer hardening is allowed to proceed and the more micelles bond, the more difficult it will be to get moisture out of the resultant curd during drainage. For this reason, when making a hard cheese, it is advantageous to have a soft gel at cutting; for soft cheese, a hard gel is preferable.

THE SPEED OF COAGULATION

The coagulation speed is dependent upon a number of factors:

Acidity Lower pH at renneting reduces the flocculation time.

Calcium The addition of calcium to the milk shortens the hardening time. Calcium chloride is sometimes used to improve the curd firmness and yield, but it is not without its problems and can lock in more moisture. I try to avoid it.

Temperature Hardening is slow or not seen at temperatures below 20°C/68°F, increasing in speed at temperatures of up to 40°C/104°F.

Protein Increased protein content in the milk shortens the hardening time.

Species Sheep's milk will flocculate faster and harden more quickly than cow's milk so the ratio of hardening time to flocculation should be reduced. Goat's milk, however, shows weak coagulation properties and the hardening time should thus be increased.

Diagram of Coagulation

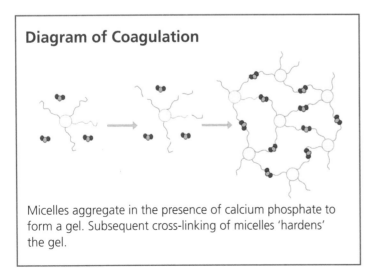

Micelles aggregate in the presence of calcium phosphate to form a gel. Subsequent cross-linking of micelles 'hardens' the gel.

This book details the expected flocculation and hardening times for each of the recipes. If the flocculation time for the milk that you are using is markedly different, the hardening time should be modified proportionally. For example, a recipe predicts a flocculation time of 20 minutes and a hardening time of 40 minutes, which is two times the flocculation time, so the cut takes place 60 minutes after the addition of the rennet. If the milk flocculates faster, in 15 minutes for example, the hardening time should be reduced to 30 minutes and the cut would take place just 45 minutes after addition of the rennet, but the curd would be just as firm. Flocculation times are best kept in the region of 10–20 minutes; the dose of rennet can be decreased or increased slightly if the flocculation occurs outside these times. Curds are ready once they can be cleanly cut with a knife or finger.

HOW TO ADD THE RENNET

Many authors insist that rennet should be diluted by an equal or greater quantity of cold water prior to its addition to the milk. However, during the course of hundreds of cheese-makes, with vats varying in volume from 20–2,200 litres/5¼–581 US gallons,

opposite below: **Some cheeses use no rennet at all to achieve coagulation. Lactic curds can be coagulated by acidity, ricotta by heat and paneer, shown here, by a combination of the two.**

above left **Using a knife, test the curd for a clean break prior to cutting it.**

above right **There is no need to dilute rennet with any kind of water; it can be added directly to milk that has reached the required temperature, then stirred in for up to 10 seconds.**

I have seen this to be false. It may be true for double- and triple-strength rennet, but with standard- or reduced-strength rennet it is not difficult to disperse the coagulant before the first signs of coagulation. I, therefore, add the rennet directly to the milk, conveniently avoiding the anxiety that some people seem to have about inactivating the rennet with chlorinated water. If you are going to dilute rennet, do so just before using it. Following this method, I've found no significant difference in activity when using bottled water or chlorinated tap water.

Diluted or not, stir the rennet into the milk for up to 10 seconds before leaving it undisturbed to set. A commercial-size vat may be stirred for 3–4 minutes, but it takes much less time for the small quantities of milk used by the home cheesemaker.

pH and Acidity

I was once asked to write a few words of wisdom for a website aimed at amateur cheesemakers. 'Pay attention to pH...' I began, because this is one of my golden rules in cheesemaking, for reasons I went on to explain, and which I will cover again here.

First and foremost, the measurement of acidity is one of the principal ways in which skilled professional cheesemakers, and indeed anyone making cheese, can satisfy themselves that they have controlled the risk that they could make people who eat their produce sick. To view pH solely as a food-safety parameter, though, is to ignore the fundamental influences that it has in every aspect of the character of a cheese, namely:

- The speed with which curd coagulates; a lower pH at the coagulation stage shortens the setting time.
- The drainage of whey; lower-pH cheese will tend to retain more moisture.
- The retention of calcium; low-pH cheeses will lose more calcium in the whey, decreasing elasticity.
- The activity of ripening enzymes and ripening microflora.

The pH meter is a relatively modern invention; cheese was made for thousands of years without it. However, this does not mean that prior to the meter's invention acidity wasn't monitored. The taste and feel of the curd alone can provide an experienced cheesemaker with a lot of information about the acidification, and with knowledge handed down from generation to generation it was possible for people to learn how to make great cheese even without them understanding the exact biochemistry of the processes involved. Without this benefit of years of experience or the ability to control the quality of the milk, however, the home cheesemaker needs to measure pH in order to understand the process.

MEASURING PH

Acids, such as lactic acid, produce hydrogen ions and this is what pH measures. The results are given in values ranging from 14.00, which is highly alkaline, to 1.00, which is very acidic. Water is neutral at about pH 7.00 while fresh cow's milk is usually about pH 6.60. It is a logarithmic scale, which means that for every 1.00 pH drop, the concentration of hydrogen ions increases by a factor of 10. At pH 5.60, there is around 10 times more lactic acid than is present in milk. By pH 4.60, the concentration of lactic acid has increased by another factor of 10, so there is 100 times the amount present in milk. For that reason, even very small differences in the curd's pH during drainage from one make to the next can produce big changes in the finished cheese and, unless you were monitoring pH, you will probably struggle to work out why one batch worked and one batch didn't.

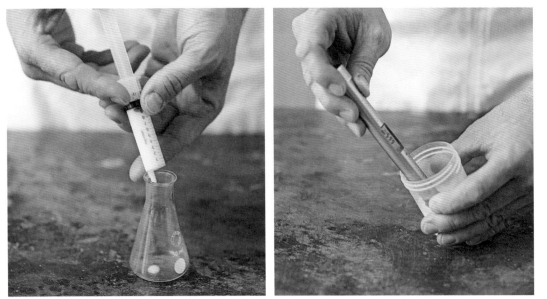

far left **A 10ml sample of whey is used to test titratable acidity. Drops of phenolphthalein indicator will be added before the sample is then titrated against 0.111 molar sodium hydroxide.**

left **To take a pH reading, collect some milk or whey in a beaker or other suitable container. Now simply dip the meter into the sample and read off and record the figure displayed on the meter.**

TITRATABLE ACIDITY

Among makers of the so-called 'Territorial' cheeses in the UK (Cheshire, Cheddar, Lancashire, Caerphilly) it is common not to describe acidity in terms of pH, but instead to use Titratable Acidity (TA), which gives results as a percentage of lactic acid. TA is a measure of the total quantity of lactic acid present in conjunction with the buffering ability of the casein. It cannot be converted directly into pH since this does not take into account the buffering effect of the casein. TA is not used much across the rest of Europe, where Dornic degrees and Soxhlet-Henkel degrees are more common.

To obtain the TA, a 10ml sample of milk or whey is placed in a small dish with two or three drops of phenolphthalein indicator. 0.111 molar sodium hydroxide is dripped into the sample (titrated) from a glass column called a burette. The titration continues until the 'endpoint' is reached, when the colour changes to pink. The quantity of sodium hydroxide added is read from a scale on the burette. This volume is equal to 10 times the percentage of lactic acid.

Titratable acidity is not without its problems for the home cheesemaker: differences in the protein content between one milk type and another will have an impact upon the TA; determination of the endpoint colour change is highly subjective; and the sodium hydroxide can deteriorate with time. For some cheeses it can also be hard to get enough whey to make up a 10ml sample. Since a pH meter can easily be used for all the recipes in this book, I will concentrate on pH alone.

If you really want to learn a lot about cheesemaking, it pays to record the pH values over time during each cheese-make and to refer back to them when tasting the ripened cheese. For me, plotting the pH values on a graph can make interpretation easier than it would be were I to look at a list of numbers.

HOW TO USE A PH METER

You will need a pH meter accurate to ±0.01 of a pH point. It doesn't need to be particularly expensive – I've tested some cheaper meters and compared them against more expensive professional ones, and the former gave good results. pH value is dependent on temperature so it is best to buy a meter with an inbuilt thermometer that compensates for this.

Taking a reading is simple: place the electrode in a sample of whey and the meter will display the pH of the sample. It is possible, with some meters, to sample the curd directly but this can slightly increase the risk of damage to the electrode. Sampling the just-drained whey gives reliable results.

Calibration should be carried out with some pH 7.00 and 4.00 buffers. Be sure to keep the probe tip hydrated and store it in some pH 4.00 or storage buffer when it is not in use. After use, immediately rinse the meter in warm water and wash it in warm soapy water at the end of the make. I tend to avoid commercial electrode-cleaning products but, if you decide to use them, dip the electrode for only a few minutes, then rinse and soak it in buffer solution for at least an hour afterwards.

Change the buffers periodically. If the reading starts to jump around or takes a long time to settle it may be that it is time to change the pH electrode. With careful handling, I've been able stretch the working life of an electrode to about 12 months.

pH Comparison for Several Cheese Varieties

	pH	Concentration of hydrogen ions (mol/litre)
Water	7.00	0.00000010
Milk	6.60	0.00000025
Cheddar curd at milling	5.40	0.00000398
Gouda at unmoulding	5.20	0.0000063
Brie at unmoulding	4.80	0.0000158
Lactic curd at ladling	4.60	0.0000251
Vinegar	2.50	0.00316

Salting and Brining

Salting is an important part of the cheesemaking process: it helps to draw excess moisture out of the curds and contributes to food safety in the finished cheese by making the remaining moisture less accessible to bacteria. It also has an inhibitory effect on the activity of the starter cultures, which helps to prevent the pH from dropping lower than the desired target, which is why you should not salt cheeses that have not yet acidified. Salting also has a major role in the correct ripening of cheese and its flavour development.

While it may be possible to reduce the salt level in low-pH fresh cheeses, reducing the quantity of salt or using sodium-replacement salts, such as magnesium or potassium, can have detrimental effects on the quality of long-aged cheeses. These include bitterness in under-salted cheeses, as well as food-safety implications ranging from an increased risk of pathogen growth to the increased production of histamine.

TYPES OF SALT

Personally, I'm not quite convinced by the use of sea salt in cheesemaking. These are sometimes marketed as being a 'low-sodium alternative', so logically we could expect to encounter similar problems to those caused by using sodium-replacement salts. Pure Dried Vacuum (PDV) salt is most commonly used for salting cheese in the UK, where salt is currently not routinely iodized. In other countries, seek out non-iodized salt if necessary.

Salt will absorb humidity from the air so store it in a lidded container to keep it dry; it will flow more evenly. Damp salt can be dried out in the oven at 130°C/266°F/Gas ¾. For surface salting, a salt shaker or a small cheese mould can be used to produce an even distribution, or you can sprinkle it on by hand.

SALTING METHODS

The three methods of salting cheese are:

Dry-salting of milled curds This method is suitable for hard cheeses including Cheddar and Cheshire. Curds are milled at a specified acidity then salt is mixed in as a percentage of the weight of curd, usually about 2 per cent. NB this may be written as '2 per cent w/w', a chemistry abbreviation that stands for 'weight to weight ratio', and one that is used in this book.

Dry-salting of the cheese surface Once a cheese has been drained and unmoulded, dry salt can be sprinkled or rubbed on its surface. This method is usually used on soft and lactic cheeses or relatively small harder varieties, since salt uptake is slow and it can be difficult to get sufficient salt into larger hard cheeses.

Brining The most common salting method used for many Continental-style hard cheeses, such as Gouda and Parmesan, is placing them in a brine tank. Here, the cheeses will float, so it is necessary to turn them over periodically during the brining to ensure even salt penetration. The immersion time is related to the size and surface area of the cheese. The cheeses may then be removed from the brining tank to be matured elsewhere.

left **Milling and salting of drained cheese curds in the production of Stilton-style cheeses is essential to prevent over-acidification, to promote ripening and to allow the pigmentation of the blue moulds.**

above right **Dry-salting of a cheese's surface is most suitable for soft and lactic cheeses, or small harder ones. You can simply sprinkle on the salt, or use your fingers to rub it evenly over the surface of the cheese.**

For cheeses that are matured in brine, such as feta, the salt percentage of the brining solution may be lower, but the contact time is longer.

Once made, brines are not usually discarded and replaced after every make, although keeping them going will require some careful handling. Brine tanks should be kept at about 12°C/54°F. Since some salt will be lost from the brine with each batch of cheese, it should be replenished every time. The exact quantity of salt will depend on the cheese type in question, but should be about 15g/½oz per 1kg/2¼lb of cheese brined. If you are going to be doing a lot of brining, it is best to periodically check the salt level of the brine solution using a floating salometer; the reading should show the solution to have at least 80 per cent salt saturation.

After using the brine tank, stir it up and strain off any solids. Don't be too surprised if the tank starts to look a little cloudy or takes on a more green-yellow colour over time. This will be diluted when the tank is topped up with liquid, an inevitable eventual occurrence since some brine is likely to be spilt each time the cheeses are removed. To top up the tank, make up a small volume of fresh brine, no more than about 10 per cent of the volume of the old brine, and add this to the tank.

HOW TO MAKE A BRINE TANK

The vinegar balances the pH and the calcium chloride is required to prevent slimy rind defects (see Troubleshooting on pages 198–9). It is possible to substitute for both by adding 250–475ml/8–16fl oz of acid-whey, such as that from the fresh curd recipe.

0.985kg/2lb 3oz salt
3.79 litres/1 US gallon water
12.5ml/2½ tsp 30–33 per cent calcium chloride solution
5ml/1 tsp vinegar

In a large lidded plastic container or bucket, combine all of the ingredients and stir until the salt dissolves.

Rind Types and Coatings

The hard cheeses covered in the recipe section of this book show a variety of different rind-styles and coatings, but these all serve essentially the same purpose: to control moisture-loss from the cheese as it matures and to protect them. Some of the following rinds and coatings are used for the recipes in this book, while others are not but are described for interest.

LARDED AND CLOTH-BOUND

The cheeses are first smeared with lard (rendered pork fat) or butter if the former is not available (or not liked), then wrapped completely in cheesecloth, which encourages the formation of a rind. Natural moulds grow upon the cheesecloth as the cheese matures, and the cloth is then removed before the cheese is eaten. This is the most common coating method used for many traditional British hard cheeses, such as Cheddar, Cheshire and Lancashire.

WAXED

Some hard cheeses are dipped in molten wax to seal the rind. Since the wax is impermeable to moisture, the cheese paste tends to stay wet, and for this reason I do not recommend it.

PLASTIC CHEESE-COATED

This coating, such as Plasticoat® or VIPLAST, is best described as food-safe 'glue' that is painted on the outside of the cheese, preventing excessive rind-drying but allowing moisture loss and gas-permeability. It is commonly found on Gouda and Parmesan.

OILED

Cheeses such as Manchego are sometimes oiled on the surface, with olive oil in this case, to exclude moulds and retain moisture. This may be carried out in conjunction with another treatment, such as plastic cheese-coating.

TOXIC MOULDS AND CHEESE RECOVERY

Many moulds have the ability to produce mycotoxins – even *Penicillium roqueforti* has been shown to produce the toxin *Roquefortine C*. Unlike meat, cheese does not seem to make a good medium for moulds to produce hazardous levels of toxin but the possibility cannot be ruled out completely and *P. roqueforti*, in spite of hundreds of years of apparently safe use, still has not been given Qualified Presumption of Safety (QPS) status by the European Food Safety Authority.

One of the less desirable mould species, *Aspergillus flavus* can produce aflatoxins, which are powerful carcinogens. A temperature of 15°C/59°F has been proposed as one below which this species is unlikely to grow and produce toxins, so it would be wise to stick to this as a maximum and store your cheese accordingly. Should a cheese display unexpected moulds having been stored above this temperature, it would be best to cut off the mouldy parts before eating it.

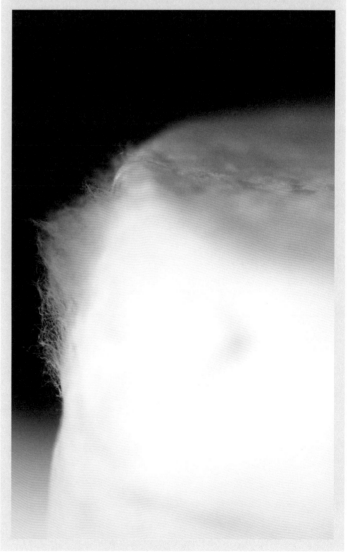

opposite left **Larded and cloth-bound cheese such as Lancashire display an impressive amount of surface mould after maturation.**

opposite right **Galette des Templiers is washed in *marc* (Pomace Brandy)** and olive oil and dusted with paprika before being mould-ripened.

above **Natural moulds such as *Chrysosporium*, *Sporondonema* and *Acremonium* pepper the rind of the hard sheep's-milk cheese Berkwell.**

SMEAR-RIPENED

The hard mountain-style cheeses such as Gruyère and Emmental are often brine-washed during their early maturation, before being brushed to create the rind typical of cheeses such as Comté. (See Mould-ripening and Rind-washing on pages 42–5.)

NATURAL MOULD

For some cheeses, such as tomme and Saint Nectaire, natural moulds are allowed to grow on the surface of the cheese. Commonly encountered moulds include the grey-brown ones of the genus *Mucor* as well as white and blue-green *Penicillium*, and *Scopulariopsis*, a white or brown mould that can 'mine' into the paste of the cheese, causing discolouration as it grows.

VACUUM-PACKED

Not one for traditionalists, vacuum-packing is most commonly used for block Cheddar but, in the absence of adequate ripening conditions and with domestic vacuum-packing machines now available on the market, some home cheesemakers may find it a useful last resort.

Mould-ripening and Rind-washing

The recipes described in the chapter on surface-ripened and blue cheese are a little more complicated than those found earlier in the book. It is not that the physical act of cheesemaking is considerably more difficult but that, for these cheeses, the subtle balance of drainage versus acidification and the tolerance of changes in humidity or temperature control can be much less forgiving. These can also be higher-risk cheeses, with more moisture and a higher pH at the end of ripening.

To meet the specific requirements of these cheeses we really need to understand the microbial populations that will progressively colonize the cheese, driving it on towards a state of perfect ripeness – or not, as sometimes happens.

Listed below are the common players in the successive stages of microbial development that occurs in surface-ripened and blue cheeses.

LACTIC ACID BACTERIA

The young cheese is first colonized by the lactic acid bacteria present in the starter culture. These bacteria produce lactic acid, reducing the pH of the environment and making it harder for other organisms to grow.

YEASTS

Fast-growing and tolerant of low pH, the yeasts are the first microbes to grow on the rind of Brie, Camembert, lactic and washed-rind cheeses and in the paste of blue cheeses. Yeasts such as *Geotrichum*, *Debaryomyces*, *Kluyveromyces* and *Yarrowia* consume lactic acid as a food source and in so doing raise the pH of their environment and make it more hospitable to other ripening organisms. At the same time they contribute protease, peptidase and lipase enzymes, which help to ripen the cheese. *Geotrichum*, in association with other yeasts, is responsible for the vermiculated 'wrinkly-brain' appearance sometimes seen on the rind of traditional Brie de Meaux, Saint-Marcellin and Langres. Yeasts grow at temperatures above 10°C/50°F and at a minimum relative humidity (RH) requirement of 88 per cent.

MOULDS

The moulds commonly encountered on cheese are *Penicillium roqueforti* in the paste of blue cheeses, and *Penicillium candidum* on the surface of Camembert-style cheeses. Others include *Mucor* and *Scopulariopsis*, which can be desirable on the surface of a natural-rind cheese but may be considered spoilage organisms if they occur on the surface of a Camembert. This is because moulds can be strongly proteolytic, breaking down the paste of the cheese and in some cases contributing to bitterness.

In addition to growing at temperatures that allow the growth of yeast, moulds also grow at temperatures below 10°C/50°F. They have lower moisture requirements than yeasts and can grow at RH levels above 60–70 per cent. They are slower-growing than yeasts or bacteria, though like yeasts they can be tolerant of low pH.

left **The classic 'wrinkly brain' appearance of some cheeses, such as Valençay, is caused by the presence of *Geotrichum* and other yeasts.**

right **Surface mould-ripened cheeses such as these doughnut-shaped ones, Rouelle, have a low pH at unmoulding, that increases after a period of 'hastening'.**

BACTERIA

The principal bacteria associated with surface-ripened cheeses include species of *Brevibacterium, Micrococcus, Arthrobacter, Microbacterium, Corynebacterium* and non-pathogenic strains of *Staphylococcus,* such as *S. xylosus*. Several of these are available as ripening cultures, though what is often sold as '*Micrococcus*' is actually *S. xylosus* and what may be available as '*Corynebacterium*' is actually *Brevibacterium*. To confuse matters further, one of the commercially available strains of *B. linens* has subsequently been determined to be *B. aurantiacum*. We shouldn't worry ourselves too much, however – they occupy a similar ecological niche and they perform in similar ways on the surface of a cheese.

Bacteria are more demanding and less resilient than yeasts or moulds but they are also faster-growing. They require a pH above 6.00 and a RH of more than 90 per cent. Growth for most ripening bacteria is possible at temperatures above 10°C/50°F.

Being tolerant of high pH, the build-up of high levels of ammonia during ripening, either in the cheese store or trapped within the packaging of a cheese, tends to promote bacterial growth. Like moulds, they are also proteolytic and the release of amino acids leads to the production of more ammonia and more rapid ripening.

We will now look at how these microbes interact in the various ripened cheese varieties.

SURFACE MOULD-RIPENED CHEESE

Brie and Camembert are soft cheeses with a very low pH at unmoulding. The yeasts are the first organisms to grow on the surface, encouraged by 'hastening' – a period of time spent in a temperature- and humidity-controlled environment. The yeasts consume lactic acid, raising the pH of the surface. The reduced level of lactic acid at the surface creates a diffusion gradient that draws more lactic acid out from the core, subsequently raising the pH there.

Moulds, inoculated into the milk before production, then begin to grow on the surface of the cheese, releasing proteolytic enzymes. These help to break down the casein structure of the paste and the metabolism of released amino acids creates ammonia as a by-product, raising the pH.

The combined action of yeasts metabolizing the lactic acid and the formation of ammonia cause the pH to rise; first at the

MEASURING HUMIDITY

I chose to omit references to relative humidity in the recipes because of the limitations in the ability to monitor it, preferring to create small microclimates for the ripening cheeses through the use of upturned plastic containers.

Digital hygroscopes can be incredibly inaccurate, their readings often drifting far above the actual humidity. My preferred method for monitoring humidity is to use a 'sling psychrometer', sometimes referred to as a 'whirling hygrometer' that is based on two thermometer bulbs – one covered in a wet sleeve, the other dry. It delivers accurate results every time but is not a method that lends itself well to the small refrigerator of a home cheesemaker.

For cheesemakers who prefer to use a digital hygroscope, accepting its limitations, the important figure to remember is 90 per cent. Below this level of relative humidity, moulds will grow and above it yeasts and bacteria will grow.

rind and then progressively at the core. Under these conditions, bacterial growth becomes possible and the late stages of ripening in Brie and Camembert are characterized by the browning of the rind, which may become sticky or slimy to the touch, and the inhibition of the slow-growing yeasts.

Holding these cheeses at too high a temperature for too long causes them to ripen too quickly, encouraging bacterial growth and the production of ammonia, which results in the browning of the rind.

WASHED-RIND CHEESE
While the pH of many washed-rind cheeses, such as Reblochon, is a little higher at unmoulding than that of Camembert, the yeasts are still the first organisms to grow on the cheese's surface. Once again, this is encouraged by a period of hastening during which the yeasts begin to consume lactic acid, raising the pH of the cheese.

Moulds are inhibited by the physical act of washing the surface of the cheese, which disrupts their growth. The combined action of yeasts metabolizing the lactic acid and the neutral pH of the wash solution raises the acidity of the rind quickly and fast-growing bacteria take the competitive advantage.

These bacteria are strongly proteolytic, leading to the production of ammonia, the presence of which further raises the pH of the cheese so that it becomes necessary to chill the cheese to slow down bacterial activity.

Failure to hasten these cheeses and too cool a ripening temperature gives the competitive advantage back to moulds. This is why Saint Nectaire is ripened at 8–9°C/47–48°F, which is cooler than the ripening conditions for most washed-rind cheeses. In the absence of bacterial competition, *Mucor* and other natural moulds take precedence.

INTERNALLY MOULD-RIPENED (BLUE) CHEESE
The ripening of blue cheeses follows a process similar to that of the surface mould-ripened ones, but the yeasts and moulds begin to grow internally, rather than externally, along lines of curd weakness (Stilton) or in pockets opened by gas production in the paste (Roquefort). Additionally, Stilton shows bacterial growth on the outer surface similar to that of a washed-rind cheese and may be considered a hybrid of the two ripening systems. Gorgonzola is also washed on the outside to encourage bacterial growth, though Roquefort is tightly wrapped in foil to discourage development of a rind.

Piercing the cheese with sterilized skewers is necessary to introduce oxygen to the paste, which allows the *Penicillium* to produce pigmented spores.

above left **Surface mould-ripened cheeses have a distinctive rind.**

above right **Mould grows in pockets in the cheese paste for this blue variety.**

right **There is a dazzling array of different types of cheeses, due in no small part to the action of microbes as well as how the cheeses are produced and matured.**

BREVIBACTERIUM LINENS AND WASHED-RIND CHEESES

Contrary to received wisdom, the surface smear of a washed-rind cheese is not dominated by *Brevibacterium linens* and several studies have failed to find it on the rinds of these cheeses even when it had been added deliberately by the cheesemaker. Instead their rinds are dominated by a complex community of bacteria and yeasts, with *Arthrobacter* being commonly reported in high numbers – even when it was not deliberately added.

Some of the more eagle-eyed readers may notice that many of the washed rind cheeses in this book include a dose of *B. linens*. Does this reflect some vested interest? The recent acquisition of shares in Europe's leading *Brevibacterium* laboratory perhaps? No. *B. linens* and *B. casei* contribute to proteolysis, and the resulting release of amino acids is important for rind pigmentation; its absence from the rind of the finished cheese does not mean that it did not serve a purpose during maturation. Perhaps, like yeast, *Brevibacterium* is best considered a pathfinder organism, one that paves the way for rind development and the proliferation of indigenous ripening bacteria.

Ironing Cheese

The cheese iron is not really an essential tool for the home cheesemaker but it does allow decisions to be made about the readiness of some types of cheese and the humidity and temperature conditions required for their further maturation, so you may wish to consider purchasing one. It could be especially useful for the hard and blue cheeses, enabling a core of cheese to be inspected without cutting it open.

Whether your cheese is graded using a cheese iron or by cutting it, make careful notes of your observations about the texture, aroma and flavour – preferably on the same page as the notes taken during the make. Linking information gathered during production to the qualities of the finished cheese is one of the best ways to develop a more advanced understanding of cheesemaking as a whole.

1 Continental-style cheeses, such as Gruyère, may be tapped on their surface with the handle of the cheese iron. Hollow sounds may be indicative of gas defects within the cheese.

2 Push the cheese iron into the side of the cheese. You will need to apply steady pressure.

3 Turn the handle 360 degrees and slowly draw out the core of the cheese. Do not try to 'drill' out the core by turning it more, and take your time over it.

4 Check the back of the cheese iron for fat distribution. For Cheddar-style cheeses, the fats should be evenly distributed. For Cheshire-style ones, the back of the iron should show less deposited fat.

THE ROLE OF THE *AFFINEUR*

The *affineur,* translated from the French for 'refiner', is responsible for the careful maturation of cheese after production, ensuring that the conditions are right for the proper flavour development of the cheese. *Affinage* can be considered to be 'the icing on the cake' – and no amount of quality icing can disguise a badly made cake!

In France, an *affineur* collects cheese from small artisan producers, some of whom may not have the maturation space to age cheeses for any length of time. After careful maturation, the *affineur* distributes the cheeses for sale, allowing the cheesemaker to concentrate on making exceptional cheese.

a   b   c

5 Reserving the outer end of the core, break off the tip. Work it in your fingers to warm and soften it, releasing volatile flavour compounds. Assess the texture of the cheese while working the paste.

6 Smell the cheese and taste it, noting down your observations. Replace the core of the cheese into the hole and use some of the cheese reserved from the grading to seal the gaps around the hole and core, in order to prevent excessive growth of blue moulds.

7 Keep your cheese iron in good condition; it should be washed after use in hot, soapy water, rinsed well and dried before being put away.

d

e

f

Wrapping Cheese

There are several options for the home cheesemaker when it comes to materials that can be used to wrap cheese. Cheesemaking equipment suppliers will usually stock a few options from the list.

POLYPROPYLENE WRAP

This plastic film is available perforated or unperforated. It is good for retaining gooey soft cheeses once they have been cut or for maturing ripened lactic cheeses to stop them drying out.

WAXED PAPER

This type of paper is useful for wrapping hard and semi-hard cheeses, blue varieties, washed-rind cheese and Camembert-style types. It is quite versatile and is recommended in several of the recipes in this book.

Lightweight waxed papers can become soggy if wet cheeses are packed into them and it can also be hard to separate soft cheeses from the paper after extended storage.

DUPLEX PAPER

A good option, this is a thin plastic film laminated to a paper outer. I've seen improved rind pigmentation on some washed-rind cheeses when they have been wrapped in duplex paper. Wetter cheeses will seep moisture out to the paper layer, causing it to deteriorate, but it is otherwise fairly versatile.

FOIL

Ordinary household or catering aluminium foil is no good for many soft and blue cheeses as it becomes corroded over time. Use a foil designed for cheese use that has been coated on the inside. These foils are typically used for storing blue cheeses.

CLEAR FILM OR PLASTIC WRAP

This is not a good option for many cheese types since it causes them to 'sweat' and retain moisture. A layer of clear film over the cut face of the cheese (but not the rind) can help to keep it in good condition but do not encase the whole block in clear film or plastic wrap.

In the absence of a suitable foil this may be the next best option for the Roquefort-style cheeses, helping to retain moisture and minimizing surface moulding.

GREASEPROOF PAPER

This is not quite as good as cheap waxed paper but is a reasonable fall-back if nothing else is available.

left **There are many different ways of wrapping cheese, depending upon their type. For this 'Little Colonel', which I developed in association with James's Cheese, a combination of polypropylene wrap and raffia string looks attractive as well as being appropriate.**

HOW TO WRAP CHEESE IN PAPER

When wrapping whole cheeses, before or after they have been cut open, place the cheese in the middle of a square of paper, gather the two opposite sides together so they meet in the middle at the top and fold them over together in a neat ridge so that the paper is flush with the top of the cheese. Fold each of the remaining open edges into triangle shapes, rather like wrapping a birthday present, bring them up to the top and then turn over the cheese so the flaps are underneath. The weight of the cheese will stop the wrapping from opening. The cheese should be firmly but not tightly encased in the paper.

For soft cheeses such as Camembert and Brie, cut a square of paper that is nearly twice the width of the cheese. Place the cheese in the middle of the paper and fold over one corner to partially enclose the cheese. Turn the cheese and paper about 45 degrees and fold another flap of paper in towards the centre, locking down the first fold. Continue turning the cheese and folding the paper in this way until the cheese is fully wrapped and enclosed in the paper. Secure the final fold with some adhesive tape or a label or, if these are not to hand, simply turn over the cheese so that the flaps are all underneath and are secured by the weight of the cheese itself.

Larger ripened lactic cheeses may be wrapped in the same way as soft cheeses such as Camembert or Brie, but very small soft cheeses are best wrapped in the same way as the larger, harder ones. Place the cheese in the middle of a square of paper, gather the opposite sides of the paper and fold them together neatly. Fold the remaining ends into a triangle shape and bring them up to the top to form a 'parcel' of cheese. Turn over the cheese to secure the folds underneath using the weight of the cheese itself. Be careful not to pull the paper too tight as this can crush very soft cheeses.

For wedges, cut a square of paper that is nearly twice the width of the cheese. Gather the opposing sides of a square of paper and fold them together twice, which should reduce the gap between the top of the cheese and the paper and bring the edges of the fold down to the top surface. To make the finished package as neat as possible, try to angle the first folds so that they are parallel with the angle of the cheese wedge. Fold the remaining loose ends into triangles, again like wrapping a birthday present, and fold them back underneath the cheese. The weight of the cheese will 'lock' the wrapping shut but it could also be secured with some adhesive tape or a label.

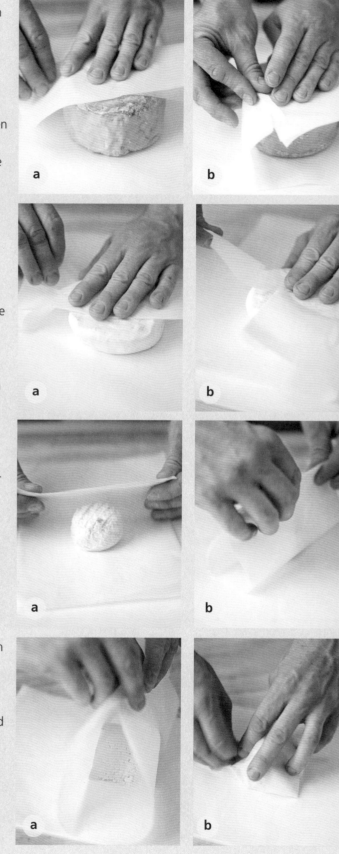

SOME EASY DAIRY PRODUCTS TO BEGIN WITH...

In this chapter we will start by experimenting with some dairy products that can be prepared quickly and easily at home, in some cases without any special equipment or ingredients.

Butter-making is so simple that many of us have accidentally started to make Sweet Cream Butter before by over-whisking cream. This chapter includes a recipe for this, as well as Cultured Butter, in which starter bacteria are used to partially acidify the cream, giving it a slightly sour, nutty flavour.

Yogurt and Crème Fraîche provide an interesting introduction to using lactic acid bacteria to ferment milk or cream, and we also explore the differences between set, stirred and Greek-style yogurts.

Our first introduction to cheese comes in the form of Paneer, which is made using heat and acidity to precipitate the curd, and Cottage Cheese, which requires starter cultures, rennet and a little time to set the curd, but is well worth the wait.

Yogurt

Rich and creamy, home-made yogurt has multiple uses in the kitchen and can be prepared the day before you plan to enjoy it. There are several types: stirred or Swiss yogurt; strained yogurt; and set yogurt, and to these can be added all manner of flavourings.

MAKES
about 500ml/17fl oz

YOU WILL NEED
500ml/17fl oz whole cow's, sheep's or goat's milk
0.1 unit thermophilic yogurt starter: YC-X16 or YC-280 (Christian Hansen), YoMix 205 (Danisco) or equivalent starter containing *Streptococcus thermophilus* and *Lactobacillus delbrueckii* subsp. *bulgaricus*

EQUIPMENT
Stainless-steel pan with a lid; spoon; thermometer; 500ml/17fl oz-capacity wide-necked vacuum flask; weighing scales; large bowl; pH meter; small bowl or lidded glass jar

TIME
4–5 hours

STIRRED YOGURT

1 Pour the milk into the pan and heat it to 90°C/194°F, stirring constantly with a wooden spoon. Once this temperature is reached, remove the pan from the heat. Leave it to stand for 5 minutes with the lid on to retain the heat; this should be sufficient to denature the whey proteins.

2 Warm the vacuum flask by filling it with boiled water. Leave the flask to stand for a minute before discarding the water. Weigh out the starter in the remaining time. ▶

The process of making yogurt is straightforward but not entirely foolproof and it is a good introduction to the complexities of dairy fermentation. As is the case with cheese-making, yogurt-making requires careful temperature control and pH monitoring; many of the faults commonly reported can be attributed to neglect of one or both of these. Yogurt is made using two principal strains of thermophilic lactic acid bacteria: *Streptococcus thermophilus* and *Lactobacillus delbrueckii* subsp. *bulgaricus*, sometimes with probiotic strains, such as *Lactobacillus acidophilus* or *Bifidobacterium lactis*. Achieving the right flavour depends on the correct balance of these two organisms being used. It is also possible to make yogurt by incubating milk with some yogurt from a previous batch – usually about 2 per cent by volume – but the proportion of each starter strain will change over time, making it hard to reproduce the particular qualities of an outstanding batch.

Here, we will look at the main types of yogurt: stirred or Swiss yogurt, which can be spooned or poured out, and which can then be strained to make Greek-style yogurt; and set yogurt, which must be set in the pot in which it will be served. Both involve heating the milk to 90°C/194°F to denature all of the whey proteins. This improves the texture of the finished yogurt and, while it is possible to bypass this denaturation step, without it the yogurt can turn out thin, grainy, slimy or stringy.

a   b

3 Place the pan in a bowl of cold water to rapidly reduce the temperature. The starter can be added and stirred in once the milk reaches 45–50°C/113–122°F. Once this has been added, leave the mixture to cool to 42°C/108°F.

4 Transfer the yogurt to the vacuum flask and close the lid.

5 Leave the flask undisturbed for a couple of hours before you check the pH and temperature. The acidification should take about 3–4 hours; you are aiming for a pH of about 4.70.

6 The temperature should remain above 40°C/104°F throughout the incubation. If it falls much below that, pour the milk back into the pan and heat it back to 42°C/108°F before returning it to the flask.

7 As the yogurt nears pH 4.70, pour it out into a bowl or glass jar and stir it until the pH reaches 4.60. It should appear a little thicker at this point.

8 It is important that the yogurt begins to cool slowly to room temperature during the stirring so do not preheat the bowl or jar. You could also use a food mixer on a slow setting to stir the yogurt, though it is not difficult to do it by hand using a wooden spoon.

9 Once the pH reaches 4.60, place the bowl or jar in cold water to cool it rapidly to 5°C/41°F, which causes the acidification to stall.

10 Serve the yogurt immediately or cover the bowl or jar with some clear film or plastic wrap and store the yogurt in the refrigerator until required. It is best used within a week.

GREEK-STYLE STIRRED YOGURT

1 For a thicker style of stirred yogurt, follow steps 1–9 but strain the yogurt through a cheesecloth-lined strainer positioned over a bowl when it is in the refrigerator, to remove some of the whey. If the resultant yogurt is a bit too thick it is possible to thin it by stirring in a little of the whey.

2 Decant the yogurt into a serving bowl and enjoy immediately or store, covered, in the refrigerator for up to a week.

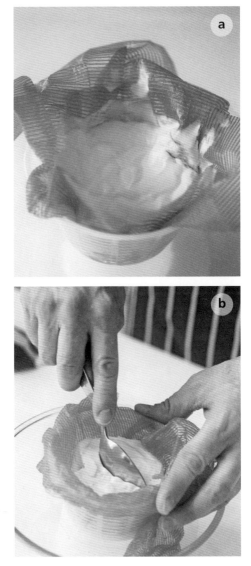

SET YOGURT

1 Follow steps 1–3 of the method for stirred yogurt, then transfer the yogurt to several small lidded jars rather than the vacuum flask for the incubation period.

2 Place the jars in a small cool box so that they fit fairly snugly. The cool box will act as insulation, retaining heat in the jars.

3 Leave the yogurt undisturbed for a couple of hours before you check the pH and temperature. The latter should remain above 40°C/104°F throughout the incubation. If it has dropped below this when you check it after a couple of hours, place some jars filled with hot water inside the cool box to act as a heat source. The acidification should take about 3–4 hours; you are aiming for a pH of about 4.60.

4 At this stage the yogurt in the jars will appear to be set and may have a drop of whey pooling about the surface or edges. Remove the jars from the box carefully to avoid damaging the yogurt gel and transfer them to the refrigerator until you are ready to serve the yogurt.

THE FLAVOUR OF YOGURT

The characteristic 'yogurt' flavour is a result of the production by the starter bacteria of lactic acid and aromatic compounds. The principal aromatic compounds are: acetaldehyde or ethanal, which imparts a flavour commonly described as 'green'; and diacetyl, a buttery compound that contributes balance and 'roundness' to the flavour. Production of these aromatic compounds occurs between pH 5.00 and 4.40, so a yogurt that acidifies too rapidly can have very little flavour. This range of pH values, being near the isoelectric point (see The Cheesemaking Process on pages 10–13) of milk, also influences the texture and viscosity of the yogurt, so careful monitoring of the pH can avoid a multitude of problems.

The characteristics of the individual strains in the starter also influence the acidification due to different temperature- and pH-tolerance, with *Lactobacillus delbrueckii* being more dominant in sour-tasting yogurt. *Streptococcus thermophilus* is marginally less heat-tolerant, and incubation temperatures higher than 45°C/113°F can give *Lb. delbrueckii* a competitive advantage, producing yogurt with a tart flavour and a tendency towards further acid development during storage, a process called 'post-acidification'. For the same reason, unless a strong-tasting, sour yogurt is wanted, the blend of starter bacteria is best maintained at a ratio high in *S. thermophilus*.

In addition to its natural taste, you can of course add all sorts of flavours to yogurt, too. Fruit purées such as raspberry, strawberry, gooseberry, rhubarb or apple are wonderful, or you can drizzle it with some honey, sprinkle over some crunchy granola, or stir through chunks of fresh fruit or whole berries.

Butter

Very quick to prepare, home-made butter adds something special to even the simplest of meals. Here are methods for making sweet cream butter, made just from fresh cream, as well as more flavoursome cultured (fermented) butter, made from cream and live cultures.

Making sweet cream butter involves whisking cream until the fats form solid, naturally sweet-tasting grains in a pool of buttermilk. On average, you'll get about half as much butter as the amount of cream used, plus some buttermilk. The buttermilk is then drained off; the liquid from the first draining, although different from buttermilk produced while making cultured butter, can still be used for drinking or some cooking. The grains left behind are washed and 'worked' to drive off moisture, leaving sweet golden pats of butter that can be enjoyed immediately. Cultured butter uses the same principles but involves cultures, which ferment the residual lactose and result in a more complex taste and better keeping qualities. The buttermilk is also more flavoursome.

Industrial butter-making equipment is very effective at getting moisture out of the butter, resulting in a product that is durable. Home- and farmhouse-production methods are not as efficient and the butter tends to spoil more rapidly. During storage, fatty acids in the butter are released as a result of microbial action and the flavours can become unpleasantly cheesy or take on a 'butyric' quality as a result of the formation of butanoic acid – one of the acids in the stomach that gives vomit its distinctive aroma!

If all of this puts you off following any of these recipes, pause for a moment and consider this: tiny amounts of the compounds that make old butter taste horrible make fresh butter taste more delicious. This is an important lesson to take on to cheese ripening; dairy production is a process of 'controlled spoilage' that can create incredible but eventually unbearable flavours. Control the spoilage too well and you end up with a durable product with little flavour. This may be convenient for retailers, but it means that to enjoy really amazing butter you might have to make it yourself and use it up quickly. Surplus butter can be clarified, or flavoured and then frozen.

SWEET CREAM BUTTER

YOU WILL NEED
double or heavy cream
salt (1–2 per cent by weight of butter) (optional)

EQUIPMENT
Large bowl; thermometer; electric whisk; wooden spoon (if salting); 'scotch hands' or wooden spatulas

TIME
15 minutes

1 Pour the cream into a large bowl and leave it to stand until its temperature reaches 11–12°C/52–54°F. The temperature is critical as lower ones will increase the churning time, while higher ones will result in soft grains that are difficult to work.

2 Whisk the cream using an electric whisk. The cream will start to thicken as air is incorporated into it. Just beyond the 'whipped cream' stage the butter grains will start to separate from the milky white buttermilk. At this stage (see photo 'e'), you must stop whisking immediately, so keep a close watch on proceedings.

3 Pour off and reserve this first batch of buttermilk, which can be used in baking (though not as a raising agent), and cover the butter grains in cold water. These should start to feel firmer and the water will go cloudy as more buttermilk is washed out.

a   b

▶

4 Without pressing the grains, carefully drain the buttermilk (it will probably be too watery to be of use, so you can discard this and the subsequent buttermilk produced by rinsing), and wash the grains again. If the liquid still looks cloudy after this, the washing may be repeated again.

5 Drain off the liquid and, using a spoon or clean hands, start to press and knead the butter, pouring off any liquid. The resultant butter may be enjoyed unsalted or salted. If you prefer the latter, weigh the butter and beat in 1–2 per cent by weight of salt, according to preference.

6 The butter may be shaped, if you like. Two wooden paddles, known as 'scotch hands' are traditionally used to work the butter into pats or rolls but you can just use a couple of wooden spatulas. If the butter becomes too warm, place it in the refrigerator for a few minutes to firm up.

7 Enjoy the butter immediately, or store it covered with clear film or plastic wrap in the refrigerator for a few days.

FREEZING BUTTER
If you have more butter than you will use imminently, it can be frozen for up to 1 month. Simply wrap small portions of it in clear film or plastic wrap and store them in the freezer. Thaw these as required in the refrigerator.

CULTURED BUTTER (AND BUTTERMILK)

This is more complicated than the Sweet Cream Butter and requires the use of starter cultures and a pH meter. Cultured butters keep for longer because the residual lactose is fermented out of the butter. Cultured buttermilk, which may be used like the store-bought variety, is the milky liquid released when the cream separates to give the butter grains. It is only really worth reserving the liquid when it first separates, since the buttermilk that is produced subsequently is rather watery.

YOU WILL NEED
1 litre/34fl oz double or heavy cream
0.06 units of Flora Danica (Christian Hansen) or Probat 222 (Danisco) or a similar heterofermentative mesophilic starter culture
salt (1–2 per cent by weight of butter)

EQUIPMENT
Bowl; weighing scales; wooden spoon; thermometer; pH meter; electric whisk

TIME
Several hours

1 Pour the cream into a bowl, stir in the starter and leave it, covered, to ripen for several hours at 21–22°C/70–72°F.

2 The pH will initially be about 6.60 but will decrease over time. When it reaches 5.50, immediately begin to churn the butter, following the method given for the Sweet Cream Butter recipe. Again, reserve the buttermilk when it first separates (discard the milky water that is produced during the washing of the butter grains).

FLAVOURED BUTTER

Butter is a great flavour-carrier that can easily be moulded into a log shape, sliced into individual portions and frozen. These portions can then be added to all manner of dishes, from potatoes, rice or pasta to steamed vegetables, casseroles or fish.

1 Prepare the flavouring. Herbs and spices should be finely chopped or pounded so that the shaped log can easily be sliced, and garlic is best finely minced since often the butter won't be cooked for long and large chunks of raw garlic are not always desirable.

2 Beat together room-temperature butter and the flavouring, then mound it on a piece of clear film or plastic wrap and form it into a tightly-wrapped log. Chill until firm, then slice off individual portions, wrap them and freeze.

CLARIFIED BUTTER (GHEE)

This clear yellow fat keeps better and can be heated to a higher temperature without burning than standard butter.

1 Put some unsalted butter in a heavy pan over a low heat and gently melt it. Continue to heat the butter until the water starts to evaporate. It will froth vigorously at first. When the frothing subsides, remove from the heat and scoop off any remaining froth.

2 Carefully pour out and reserve the clear oil, discarding the milk solids at the bottom of the pan. Store the fat in the refrigerator until needed.

Cream

Unctuous and delicious, cream is incredibly easy to prepare and has myriad uses in the kitchen. Double or heavy cream is the cream that floats to the surface of milk and is then skimmed off, while clotted cream – traditionally associated with south-west England – is simply baked cream.

CLOTTED CREAM

Traditionally made with raw milk by the so-called 'float-cream method', whereby cream that rises to the surface of the milk is scalded on the stove and cooled very slowly, this alternative method instead involves simply baking cream in a cool oven. The average yield will be about half as much clotted cream as double or heavy cream. For those with an old-fashioned range, the warming oven is perfect, but a conventional or fan-assisted oven may also be used. The end product's distinctive sweet, scalded flavour depends on heating the cream for a sufficient amount of time, so do check it during the cooking process.

Clotted cream will not keep very long and is best used fresh, so it is advisable not to make vast quantities unless you know that it will all be used up. I find that dishes used to package Saint Félicien cheeses, each holding about 150ml/5fl oz of cream, are perfect for clotting small batches, but you can use any ovenproof ceramic dish or dishes you have to hand.

YOU WILL NEED
350ml/12fl oz double or heavy cream

EQUIPMENT
Wide, flat and ovenproof ceramic dishes or ramekins; baking tray

TIME
3 hours or more, plus cooling time

1 Preheat the oven to 80°C/176°F. Pour the cream into the dishes or ramekins and place them on a baking tray in the oven.

2 Bake for 3 hours, or until the cream appears to form a skin that starts to wrinkle and become more yellow.

3 When the cream looks reasonably well set, allow it to cool slowly before using or storing in the refrigerator for up to 4 days.

a

b

DOUBLE/HEAVY CREAM

This process requires unhomogenized cow's milk to be cooled to a low temperature without agitation. The best results are obtained with raw milk. Jersey milk tends to yield more fat, while goat's and sheep's milk do not separate readily upon standing. If you are using rich Jersey milk, the remaining skimmed milk can be added back into a larger volume of whole milk and used for cheese-making. This is a beneficial thing to do, since skimming off the cream reduces the fat content of the milk and improves the drainage properties of the curd.

YOU WILL NEED
Unhomogenized, preferably raw, whole milk

EQUIPMENT
Glass jug or pitcher or a spigot jar; spoon (optional)

TIME
24 hours

1 Pour the milk into a glass jug or pitcher or a spigot jar and place it in the refrigerator for 24 hours to allow the cream to rise to the surface of the milk.

2 The cream will now have separated to the top and can be poured or spooned off, leaving behind semi-skimmed milk.

3 Use the cream immediately, as an accompaniment or in other recipes, or store it in a covered container in the refrigerator for 3–4 days.

Crème Fraîche

With a luxurious mouthfeel and clean, slightly soured flavours, crème fraîche makes a delicious accompaniment to many puddings and is a very useful ingredient. Mascarpone is essentially strained, thickened crème fraîche and is a key ingredient in dishes such as tiramisù.

Some supermarket crème fraîche can be disappointing – thin and flavourless. Good crème fraîche, on the other hand, such as that made in Isigny in northern France, is so delicious that it begs to be eaten by the spoonful. The crème fraîche produced by the recipe here is similarly delectable eaten on its own, and also performs well in cooking, being less likely to curdle than cream.

Mascarpone is commercially produced by heating and acidifying cream rather than by culturing it but here I've adapted the crème fraîche recipe to give a more flavourful and smooth-textured product. The yield of the crème fraîche will approximately match the volume of cream, whereas since mascarpone is strained, the yield will be less.

YOU WILL NEED
600ml/20fl oz double or heavy cream
0.1 unit Flora Danica (Christian Hansen) or Probat 222 (Danisco) or equivalent heterofermentative mesophilic starter

EQUIPMENT
Jar with a lid; heatproof bowl; thermometer; weighing scales; spoon; pH meter

TIME
12–24 hours

1 Pour the cream into a sterilized jar and warm it to 25°C/77°F by standing it in a bowl of warm water.

2 Weigh the starter using weighing scales and then add it to the cream once it is up to temperature. Stir it in well and put the lid on the jar.

3 Leave the jar undisturbed standing in the bowl of water in a warm room for 12 hours. Stir the mixture and check the pH every few hours for up to another 12 hours. As the cream acidifies, it will start to become quite thick.

4 When the pH has dropped to 4.70, cool the acidified cream rapidly by standing the jar in a bowl of cold water.

5 Use the crème fraîche immediately or store it, covered, in the refrigerator for up to 5 days.

e

f

g

MASCARPONE

This version is essentially crème fraîche that is strained for 24 hours to drain away some of the liquid and produce a thicker cream.

1 Acidify the cream, following steps 1–3 for making crème fraîche.

2 Scoop the acidified cream into a strainer lined with a clean square of cheesecloth. Place the strainer over a bowl in the refrigerator for 24 hours, allowing moisture to drain.

3 After this time, the cloth should contain a firm but smooth lump of mascarpone – perfect for making a tiramisù or using in another recipe.

Paneer

Sometimes known as Indian cheese, paneer is commonly associated with India and other southern-Asian cuisines. This is a quick and easy cheese to make at home and uses simple, everyday ingredients.

Paneer is an example of a directly acidified cheese. The pH drop required for making these cheeses is achieved through chemical means by the addition of citric, lactic or acetic acid. It is not a process that is suitable for making long-aged and ripened cheeses because, in the absence of lactic acid bacteria (LAB), lactose is left in the curd and this can be a good food source for less desirable microbes.

Directly acidified cheeses lack the enzymes from the LAB that are also important to the development of flavour, meaning many are rather tasteless. Paneer uses a combination of heat and acidity to set the curd rather than rennet, and has a texture that makes it ideal for frying or adding to curries and a pleasant, mild taste that is perfect for carrying spices and other flavours. In India, paneer-type cheese forms the basis of many dishes including *aloo paneer* – an aromatic potato and cheese curry.

YOU WILL NEED
5.70 litres/1½ US gallons whole cow's, buffalo's or mixed milk
150ml/5fl oz white vinegar

EQUIPMENT
Large stainless-steel pan; thermometer; wooden spoon; pH meter; strainer; square of cheesecloth; slotted spoon; 2 chopping boards; jug or pitcher, or a weight; bowl

TIME
1¼ hours

1 Pour the milk into the large stainless-steel pan, then place it over a low heat and bring it up to 90°C/194°F, stirring occasionally with a wooden spoon to prevent the milk from sticking to the base of the pan.

2 Remove the pan from the heat and sprinkle the white vinegar over the surface of the milk. Stir it in with a spoon quickly, but gently, for 1 minute. ▶

3 Leave to coagulate for 10 minutes, during which time a combination of heat and acidity precipitate the curd into small flakes. Check the pH; the addition of vinegar should have been sufficient to reduce it to between 5.00 and 5.40.

4 Allow the curd to sink to the bottom of the pan, leaving clear, greenish-looking whey. Pour off the whey and scoop the curd into a strainer lined with a square of cheesecloth using a slotted spoon.

5 Once all of the curds are in the cheesecloth, fold in the edges to form a neat parcel. Place this between two chopping boards. Put a weight, such as a jug or pitcher of water, on top of the boards. Leave to stand for 15 minutes to press out the whey.

6 Open out the cheesecloth, remove the paneer and plunge it into a bowl of cold water. Leave it for 30 minutes.

7 Remove from the water and store, covered, in the refrigerator for up to a week. When ready to use, cut the block into strips or cubes before cooking.

g

Cottage Cheese

A world away from the industrially-made versions, the clean flavour and rich mouthfeel of cottage cheese quickly repays the effort required to make it. The technique used is also a helpful stepping stone for anyone interested in experimenting with the fresh and brined cheese recipes.

YOU WILL NEED

11.4 litres/3 US gallons whole cow's milk

2 units R704 (Christian Hansen) or MA11 (Danisco) or equivalent homofermentative mesophilic starter

1ml/⅕ tsp or about 20 drops rennet of 1:10,000 strength (see page 32)

1 per cent salt (10g/¼oz per 1kg/2¼lb of curd)

double or heavy cream, to loosen the curds to the desired consistency

EQUIPMENT

Large stainless-steel pan; thermometer; wooden spoon; pH meter; weighing scales; knife; strainer; ladle; square of cheesecloth; bowl

TIME

About 10 hours

This is a cheese that is coagulated predominantly by acidification, with only a tiny amount of rennet being used. However, unlike the lactic curd recipe we will look at next, there are processing steps – including curd-cutting, stirring, heating and washing – that will encourage whey to leave the curds, which become progressively firmer before they are 'dressed' with some cream to add richness. The exact amount of cream added is a matter of judgement and preference, but about half the volume of the curd, or slightly less, might make a good starting point.

The rapid acidification and high scald temperature make this recipe a relatively safe introduction to home cheese-making. In addition to a small quantity of rennet, it uses a high dose of a fast starter that will bring down the pH to the isoelectric point (see page 83) in about 6 hours.

1 Pour the milk into a large stainless-steel pan and gently warm it over a low-medium heat until it reaches 30°C/86°F on the thermometer, stirring occasionally with a wooden spoon to prevent the milk from sticking to the base of the pan.

2 Remove the pan from the heat when the milk gets to temperature, then measure and record its pH with the pH meter.

3 Carefully weigh the starter using the weighing scales, then add it to the warm milk and stir with the wooden spoon to combine thoroughly. Leave the milk mixture to stand for 1 hour.

►

4 After 1 hour, measure the rennet and stir it in well with a spoon for a minute before leaving the curd to acidify and coagulate for about 6 hours.

5 Cut the curd when the pH reaches 4.70–4.60, at which point the milk will have set into a firm but brittle gel.

6 Using the knife, make a series of even parallel cuts spaced 1.3cm/½in apart, then turn the pan through 90 degrees and make a second series of crossways cuts with the same spacing.

7 For the final cut, hold the knife at 45 degrees to the curd and make a series of diagonal cuts.

8 Leave the cut curd undisturbed for 10 minutes for the surface of the curd particles to 'heal', during which time the curd surface becomes slightly firmer.

9 Stir the curds and begin to heat the pan in short bursts, raising the temperature 4°C/39°C degrees every 10 minutes, to reach a target of 55°C/131°F within 1 hour. Stir the curds every 5 minutes.

10 Once the target temperature is reached, stop stirring and allow the curds to sink to the bottom of the pan. Drain off the whey through a strainer.

11 Fill the pan with cold water to wash and cool the curds. Stir them briefly with a spoon, then allow them to sink back to the bottom of the pan.

12 Strain again and repeat with fresh water. The curds should have cooled to 5–10°C/41–50°F. If not, repeat the washing process until this temperature is reached.

13 Ladle the cooled curds into a square of cheesecloth placed inside a strainer. Position the strainer over a bowl and leave to drain for 10 minutes.

14 Discard the water, put the curds in the bowl and stir in 1 per cent salt by weight.

15 Pour in double or heavy cream to loosen the curds to the desired consistency.

16 Use immediately, or transfer to a lidded container. The cheese will last for up to a week stored in this way in the refrigerator.

FRESH & BRINED CHEESES

The recipes in this chapter can be very easy and take relatively little time to make, and are ready to eat immediately.

Fresh Curd simply involves straining off curds formed during the souring of milk by lactic acid bacteria, while Colwick is produced by the slow drainage of soft rennet-coagulated cheese curds through a cloth-lined mould.

Mozzarella, by comparison, poses more of a technical challenge but it is very rewarding to make, and has the added bonus that you can simultaneously create Ricotta; a 'whey cheese' that can be quickly made by precipitating the protein in the whey drained during the mozzarella make.

In comparison to 'stretchy' mozzarella, there is also a recipe for 'squeaky' Halloumi-style Cheese, the two methods illustrating the important role of acidity development in determining textural properties and 'meltability'. The brined Feta-style Cheese, meanwhile, is a delicious introduction to cheeses that require a period of maturation in order to unlock their flavour.

Fresh Curd

Fresh curds should be soft, fluffy and mousse-like, neither excessively wet nor overly dry and crumbly. Over-acidified or badly drained cheeses may be sour, but well-made ones should taste zingy, lemony and fresh. Enjoy them with crusty bread or on their own with a drizzle of honey.

YOU WILL NEED

11.4 litres/3 US gallons whole cow's, goat's or sheep's milk

1 unit R-704 (Christian Hansen) or MA-14 (Danisco) or equivalent homofermentative mesophilic starter

1ml/⅕ tsp rennet of 1:10,000 strength (or adjusted accordingly, see page 32) (optional)

1.5 per cent w/w salt: about 28g/1oz, plus extra for salting the cheese's surface (optional)

cheesemaker's ash (optional)

EQUIPMENT

Large stainless-steel pan; thermometer; wooden spoon; large plastic bucket with lid; ladle; syringe or small measuring tube; pH meter; curd-draining bag; weighing scales

TIME

Coagulation time: 12–24 hours; drainage time: up to 24–48 hours

HAND-LADLED CHEESES

It is possible to hand-ladle curds into lactic cheese moulds using the process outlined in the method for Ripened Lactic Cheese (see pages 180–3) rather than using a drainage bag, but then eaten fresh rather than ripened. Salt the surface of the drained cheeses using about 15g/½oz salt per 1kg/2¼lb of cheese, store at 4°C/39°F and use within a week.

This fresh curd and other lactic cheeses principally use acidification rather than rennet activity to coagulate the milk. For this recipe, the acidification is achieved using a mixture of lactic acid bacteria starter cultures rather than through the addition of acid, in essence mimicking what would happen in raw milk if it were allowed to sour naturally. The earliest cheeses were probably prepared in this way.

At pH 4.60 – the 'isoelectric point' of milk – the casein is at its point of least solubility so it precipitates, forming a curd that can be ladled into moulds or drained through cloth. We have the advantage of pH meters these days, but in previous times the formation of the curd would have been assessed visually with the cheesemaker looking for a solid block of curd covered with a layer of clear whey.

Lactic cheeses are at the extreme end of the soft-cheese spectrum, with the highest moisture content of any cheese variety. The acidification, usually carried out over 8–24 hours, proceeds very slowly, usually with a long lag time at the beginning during which the acidity changes little or not at all. Goat's milk tends to acidify over a shorter time.

Making this cheese can be a good starting point for beginners. The slow acidification and high moisture introduce an element of risk in terms of pathogen growth, but this is offset to some degree by the low pH of the make and its short shelf-life.

While it is possible to coagulate through acidification alone, many lactic cheeses contain a small amount of rennet to stabilize the curd and provide a source of ripening enzymes. This can cause confusion and it may be more useful to consider 'lactic cheese' as one that is coagulated predominantly, rather than entirely, by acidification.

We will start by preparing fresh cheeses, which can be moulded into balls or logs, then optionally surface-salted with or without food-grade 'cheesemaker's' ash. Ripened lactic cheeses follow the same production process as fresh ones, but the maturation conditions are more sophisticated. These are explored later in this book.

Lactic makes take place at lower temperatures than predominantly rennet-set cheeses: 21–22°C/70–72°F is typical. Try to keep the room temperature around this level to avoid sluggish acidification or poor drainage. Lactic cheeses drain relatively badly and cold draughts really slow down the process.

This methodology has been applied to goat's, sheep's and cow's milk, but the latter can be problematic. Immunoglobulins naturally present in raw cow's milk cause fats to cream off and rise to the surface during the long, slow coagulation. The worst manifestation of this, known as agglutination, is described in Troubleshooting (see pages 198–9). Skimming some fat from the milk can limit the problem, while homogenization followed by pasteurization can resolve it. Goat's milk, with its weak rennet-coagulation properties, lends itself incredibly well to lactic cheesemaking and, in common with sheep's milk, lacks the tendency to spontaneously cream.

The recipe calls for a curd-draining bag but a cotton pillowcase or a small sheet, boiled in a pan of water to sterilize it, makes a good substitute. If using a sheet, gather the four corners and tie them together so it will fit in the pan of boiling water. ▶

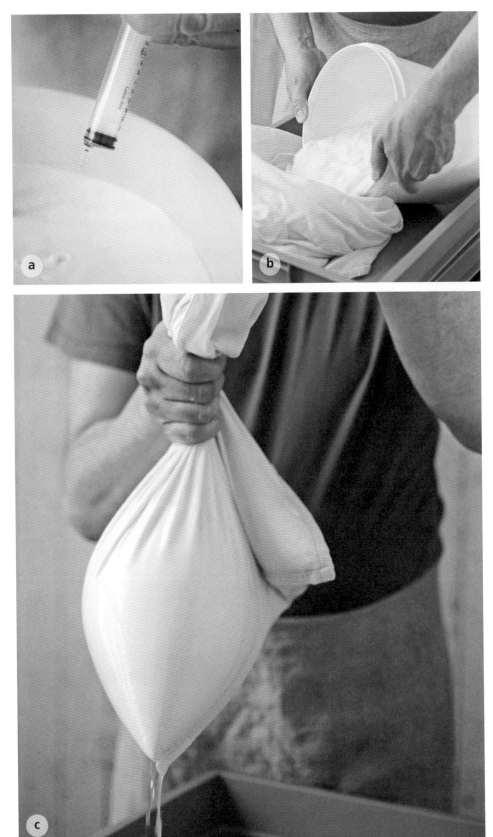

1 Pour the milk into the pan and gently heat it to 21–22°C/70–72°F, stirring continuously with a wooden spoon. Once up to temperature, transfer it to the bucket.

2 Weigh out the starter culture and stir it in. Leave for at least 10 minutes to allow the starter to rehydrate and disperse.

3 Add the rennet using the syringe or small measuring tube and stir it in. It is possible to add rennet shortly after the addition of the starter or it could be added after partial acidification, but don't add it when the pH of the milk is much below 6.30. The rennet can be omitted, though its inclusion can improve the set and drainage of the curds.

4 Cover the bucket with its lid to keep it warm and leave the milk to acidify at room temperature to pH 4.60 over 12–24 hours.

5 Weigh the empty draining bag, then pour in the curds. Tie the end and hang it up to drain over the now-empty bucket for 24–48 hours in a room at about 21–22°C/70–72°F. Shake up the curd in the bag several times during this time to improve drainage, but try to make sure that all of the bits end up at the bottom; particles left on the upper sides of the bag can dry into hard grains and spoil the finished texture.

6 Weigh the curd in the bag, deduct the weight of the empty bag, and place the curds in the cleaned bucket. Mix in 15g/½oz salt per 1kg/2¼lb of curd, stirring well to ensure even salt distribution.

7 The curds can be eaten immediately or covered and stored at 4°C/39°F for about a week. You can hand-mould them into small logs or balls or to use a moulding plate (see box on page 19).

FLAVOURED CURD CHEESES

It is common to find some shaped fresh cheeses with herbs and spices sprinkled on their surface, such as figue cheese from Provençe in the south of France, a goat's cheese shaped into a ball (or 'fig', hence its name). Garlic, chives, black pepper, thyme and other Provençale herbs, pink 'peppercorns' (*Schinus molle*) or paprika are sometimes used.

Because dried herbs and spices are often intended to be cooked rather than to be consumed raw, it is important to note that there are sometimes question-marks over the microbiological safety of using them in their uncooked state, with *Salmonella* species being a significant concern. However, heating herb mixes to at least 72°C/162°F for 15 seconds by placing them in boiling water prior to use would address the main food-safety concerns in this instance.

8 If salting the surface, you can either sprinkle over neat salt, or mix it in a ratio of 50:50 with ash and then sprinkle it over. Mixing the salt with the ash has the benefit of providing a visual aid to ensure even salting of the cheeses' surface.

9 It is also possible to sprinkle on the charcoal after the cheeses have been salted. You could make a stencil to create a pattern with the charcoal, such as the cross found on Cathare, a goat's milk cheese from the south of France.

Colwick

This soft, fresh cheese frequently appears in old cheesemaking textbooks though its production had all but died out until a few years ago, when there was a revival in interest. The town after which Colwick is named is in Nottinghamshire and is traditionally associated with the making of Stilton, Nottinghamshire being one of the three counties in England in which that famous cheese may be made. Colwick, as locals will be quick to point out, should be pronounced Col'ick rather than Cole'wick or Col'wick.

YOU WILL NEED

11.4 litres/3 US gallons whole cow's
milk

0.7 units Flora Danica (Christian Hansen)
or Probat 222 (Danisco) or equiv.
heterofermentative mesophilic starter

3.4ml/scant ¾ tsp rennet of 1:10,000
strength (or adjusted accordingly,
see page 32)

15g/½oz salt (optional)

EQUIPMENT

Large stainless-steel pan; thermometer;
wooden spoon; large plastic bucket;
weighing scales; syringe or small
measuring tube; scissors; cheesecloth;
3 small colanders; draining table or
tray; ladle; pH meter

TIME

Coagulation time: 2 hours; drainage
time: 13–25 hours

1 Pour the milk into the large stainless-
steel pan and gently warm it over a
low-medium heat to 30–31°C/ 86–88°F,
stirring continuously with a wooden
spoon. Transfer the milk to the bucket.

2 Weigh out the starter culture, then add it
to the milk and stir it in. Leave it to stand
for 1 hour, stirring occasionally to stop the
cream from rising to the surface.

3 Add the rennet using the syringe or small
measuring tube and stir it in thoroughly for
about 1 minute.

4 Leave the curd, undisturbed, for 1 hour.
The first signs of coagulation should be
noticeable after about 10 minutes but
the curd should be left to harden for
50 minutes more.

Making Colwick is a simple enough method, involving the ladling of uncut curds into a cloth-lined mould. The cloth, folded over as the curd drains, produces an unusual concave centre in the cheese. Colwick is intended to be eaten fresh, but historically it was sometimes ripened for a few days in a warm room, allowing yeasts to grow on the surface. The cheese has a satisfying acidic, curdy quality and a clean, mild flavour and I think it cries out to be served with dried fruit – some raisins or figs perhaps – or soft fruit, such as strawberries.

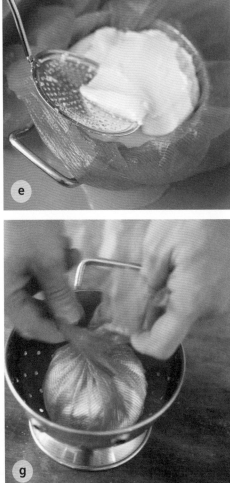

5 Meanwhile, use scissors to cut three squares of cheesecloth large enough to line the three colanders. Place these on the draining table or tray.

6 About 1 hour after the addition of the rennet, ladle the uncut curd one large scoopful at a time into the cloth-lined colanders, taking care not to damage the delicate curds. Aim to divide the curds equally between the three colanders, placing one scoop into each in turn before returning to the first to begin topping up.

7 Leave the bundles to drain in a warm room of at least 21–22°C/70–72°F for 1 hour, after which time the curds should have shrunk in the moulds.

8 Fold in the edges of the cheesecloth to release any curd that may be stuck to it and gather together three of the corners of the cheesecloth in one hand, holding them upright. Loop the fourth corner once around the other three, tucking the end underneath the loop that is formed. This is called a 'Stilton knot'. Pull the knot tight to secure the bundle of curd.

9 Continue to drain the cheeses for 12–24 hours. Do not turn them during drainage. The knot can be re-tied a little tighter if drainage is too slow. Colwick is meant to be quite soft, so do not re-tie too often as doing so can result in a dry cheese.

10 Test the pH periodically during the drainage time; it should be below 5.00 when the Colwick is unmoulded.

11 Sprinkle the salt, if using, evenly over the surface of the three cheeses and enjoy them immediately or store them, covered, in the refrigerator for up to 5 days.

Mozzarella

The sweet, milky flavour of mozzarella makes a classic pairing with basil and tomatoes. Buffalo-milk versions tend to be softer and silkier than those made from cow's milk. This recipe requires no complicated ripening, and the process of stretching the curd is particularly enjoyable.

YOU WILL NEED

11.4 litres/3 US gallons whole cow's or buffalo's milk

2.3 units ST-M7 (Christian Hansen) or TA 50 (Danisco) or equivalent *Streptococcus thermophilus* starter

2.5ml/½ tsp rennet of 1:10,000 strength (or adjusted accordingly, see page 32)

about 21g/¾oz salt (1.5 per cent of curd weight)

EQUIPMENT

Large stainless-steel pan; thermometer; wooden spoon; weighing scales; syringe or small measuring tube; kitchen knife; hand-held balloon whisk; pH meter; clean dish towel or cloth; tray or plate; heatproof bowl; lidded container

TIME

About 7 hours

This popular cheese hails from the Campania region of Italy where production of the traditional Mozzarella di Bufala Campania DOP is, as the name implies, strictly restricted to buffalo milk. The method has been copied across the world and cow's-milk versions are more often encountered than the original. If you can get hold of some buffalo milk then the results could be quite spectacular, but you must eat it very fresh (as the Italians do) for this is not a cheese that travels or ages well.

This recipe can be made in two styles: the high-moisture mozzarella balls that are often torn or sliced into tomato and basil salad, or the lower-moisture 'pizza mozzarella' that is used in cooking, though purists may frown upon the latter. The acidification, milling and salting process used for both types shares some similarities with the Cheddar cheese recipe that we will explore later in this book.

The key to success here lies in the careful monitoring of pH levels during the acidification (see pH and Acidity on pages 36–7). The curd's stretchiness is dependent on the cheese having a pH of about 5.25 before it is milled, salted and stretched; many a batch of mozzarella has been ruined when this target is overshot. Sufficient heat is also required to cause the curd to melt and enable kneading, which stretches out the casein in much the same way that kneading bread dough stretches out gluten.

Rather than using the direct acidification method, here we will be using a starter culture of thermophilic lactic acid bacteria. These bacteria will not grow below 30°C/86°F so maintaining sufficient heat in the vat will be essential and the room should be kept very warm and draught-free.

1 Pour the milk into the pan and gently heat it to 37°C/99°F, stirring continuously with a wooden spoon to prevent it from sticking and burning on the bottom of the pan. Maintaining this target temperature will be essential throughout the make so ensure you keep a close eye on it.

2 Weigh out the starter culture using the weighing scales, then add it to the milk and stir it in. Leave the milk mixture to stand for 1 hour, stirring it occasionally with a wooden spoon to stop the cream from rising to the surface. ▶

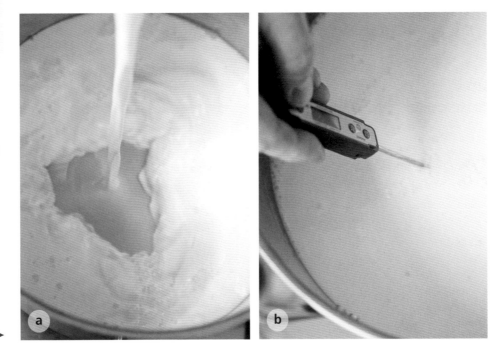
a   b

3 Check the temperature of the milk and adjust it back to 37°C/99°F if necessary by placing the pan over a low heat.

4 Measure out the rennet using the syringe or small measuring tube and stir it in thoroughly for about 1 minute.

5 Leave the curd, undisturbed, for about 50 minutes. The curd should show the first signs of setting after about 25 minutes but should be left to harden for another 25 minutes, slightly less if using buffalo's rather than cow's milk.

6 Check the curd. It should be a fairly soft gel but should break cleanly when tested with the tip of a sharp knife. Make several parallel cuts spaced about 2cm/¾in apart. Make a second series of cuts of the same spacing at 90 degrees to the first.

7 To perform the final cut, start stirring gently with the balloon whisk, breaking down the columns of curd to 1cm³/⅓in³ over the course of 15 minutes. Aim to achieve a consistent size of curds. Stop whisking and stir instead by hand if the curds become too small. You are aiming to

achieve curds that resemble cottage cheese, as shown in picture 'h'. Stirring releases whey from the curd and if this curd has been carefully cut and stirred, the whey should now be a greenish-yellow colour.

8 When stirring stops the curds should sink readily to the bottom of the pan. Leave the curd to settle for 5 minutes, then carefully pour off the whey to leave a 'cake' of curd at the bottom of the pan, taking care not to lose any of the curd. If you like, you could retain the drained whey and use it for making Ricotta (see pages 96–7).

9 Leave the curd in the pan to acidify in a warm place, turning over the 'cake' every 15–20 minutes to aid drainage.

10 Any whey that is expressed from the curd should be carefully poured off at every turn and the pH taken. The target is pH 5.25 and the acidification process should take about 4 hours in total – although it may take a little longer if the curds cool too quickly. Keep the pan warm by covering it with a clean dish towel or cloth. By this point the curd should be quite springy.

11 When the target pH is reached, immediately mill the curd by hand or using a knife on a tray or plate. Aim to break down the curds into rough but evenly sized chunks measuring 1cm³/⅓in³.

12 Weigh the curd, then calculate the required quantity of salt according to the yield of curd (see pages 38–9).

13 Measure out the required amount of salt and stir it evenly and thoroughly into the milled curds. It may be best to use your hands to do this.

14 Put the milled curds in a heatproof bowl and add 1 litre/34fl oz hot water at 95°C/203°F for every 1kg/2¼lb of milled curd and stir with a wooden spoon until the curd starts to melt into a single mass. It is normal for the water to look quite cloudy at this point.

15 Using your hands, lift out the mass and separate it into several smaller pieces of around 200g/7oz each. Stretch and shape these into balls, being careful not to overwork the curd, which would cause it to become tough and rubbery. ▶

o

p

16 Fold each curd ball in on itself until the surface is smooth and glossy. If the surface looks rough or shows signs of tearing then the curd has cooled below the melting point and it needs to be reheated by being placed in a bowl of warm water.

17 Use the mozzarella balls immediately or transfer them to a container of cool (not cold) water and put a lid on it. They are best used within a day or two (especially if made with buffalo's milk) but cow's milk ones will last for up to 5 days if stored in the sealed container in the refrigerator.

BRAIDED MOZZARELLA

Follow the method for mozzarella balls, but rather than shaping the curds into balls, instead stretch it into strands that can be braided.

PIZZA MOZZARELLA

1 This pizza or grating mozzarella is made following the same process as standard mozzarella, except that after coagulation the curd can be cut more finely, to around 5mm³/⅙in³, which will encourage moisture loss.

2 Stir the curds for 10 minutes longer in Step 8, prior to draining the whey.

3 After achieving pH 5.25 and milling, salting and stretching the curds, the mozzarella should be formed into a single mass of curd, then worked until the curd becomes firm before being cooled rapidly in a container of cool (not cold) water.

4 Wrap the block in clear film or plastic wrap and refrigerate until required. It will keep for up to 5 days.

Ricotta

Made from the sweet whey left over from making mozzarella, ricotta is very popular in Italy, where it is often mixed with chopped spinach and used as a filling in dishes such as cannelloni and ravioli. Similar whey cheeses are also produced elsewhere: Sérac is produced in Switzerland and the Savoie region of France, while Brocciu hails from Corsica and is made from sheep's or goat's whey and milk and is drained in rush baskets.

YOU WILL NEED

5.7 litres/1½ US gallons 'sweet whey' with a pH above 6.20

100ml/3½fl oz whole or full-fat milk to each 1 litre/34fl oz whey (optional)

28g/1oz salt

0.2ml/3 drops distilled malt vinegar

EQUIPMENT

pH meter; large stainless-steel pan; thermometer; wooden spoon; ricotta mould; cheesecloth; slotted spoon

TIME

1–2 hours

1 Check the pH of the whey is correct, then pour it and the milk, if using, into the pan. It is not possible to make ricotta if the whey is too acidic. Heat the liquid slowly to 85°C/185°F over a low-medium heat, stirring occasionally with a wooden spoon to prevent it from sticking.

2 Add the salt and vinegar, then stop stirring, remove the pan from the heat and leave it to stand for 5 minutes. Curds will rise like a foam to the surface and stirring at this stage can cause them to sink.

3 Line the mould with cheesecloth. Scoop the curds from the surface of the whey with the slotted spoon and transfer them to the mould.

4 Drain the curds in a cool place for 1–2 hours, until the ricotta is the desired consistency. Stir in a little of the drained whey if it is too dry.

5 Use the ricotta immediately or store it in a lidded container in the refrigerator at 4°C/39°F for up to a week.

The process of making ricotta is quite different from most of the other recipes in this book in that it is produced using heat to denature the soluble proteins from whey, which are left over following the production of other cheese varieties. The recipe calls for 'sweet whey' such as that produced after draining off mozzarella, Gruyère or Provolone cheeses. The acid whey produced during lactic coagulation cannot be used. Whey proteins only make up about 20 per cent of the total protein in milk so don't expect this recipe to yield large quantities. It is, however, possible to add up to 100ml/3½fl oz whole or full-fat milk to each 1 litre/34fl oz whey to improve the yield. Here, a ricotta mould is used but any wide, shallow soft cheese mould lined with cheesecloth should work.

After draining the whey from the mozzarella, there is plenty of time to make a batch of ricotta from the whey before the mozzarella curds are ready for stretching, so it makes perfect sense to make the two simultaneously.

a

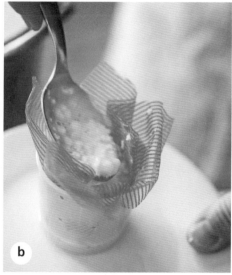

b

c

GRATING RICOTTA

Pressing, salting and leaving ricotta to dry out means it has a harder texture than standard ricotta and can be grated, crumbled or sliced.

1 Prepare the ricotta as per the recipe but place a weight on top of the cheesecloth during draining.

2 Put the formed cheese in a bowl and lightly salt its surface. Leave uncovered, and place it in the refrigerator to dry out for up to 4 weeks before use.

Feta-style Cheese

The complex salty taste and crumbly, melt-in-the-mouth texture of home-made feta-style cheese pairs well with olives or beetroot and adds bursts of intense flavour to a summer salad.

There are examples of brined cheeses from across the Mediterranean and the Balkans, but Greek feta is perhaps the best known. This is made from sheep's milk, with the permitted addition of up to 30 per cent goat's milk. The European Union approved a Protected Designation of Origin (PDO) status in 2002 so use of the term 'feta' is restricted, but the methodology is widespread and there are many examples of this type of cheese, including Telemea from Romania, Bulgarit from Israel and Sirene from Bulgaria.

I should make a distinction here between ripened cheeses that are brined as part of the production process, such as Gouda, and the acidic fresh cheeses matured in brine I am describing in this recipe. The concentration of the brine is much lower than that described in preparing a brine tank (see page 39). The make is relatively quick: the curd is coagulated and cut then placed in moulds to drain for 12–24 hours before being placed in the brine.

There are some farmhouse-style feta starters available that contain a blend of homofermentative mesophiles and thermophilic strains for improved flavour and texture. However, since the typical make temperature is not far above that required for thermophiles to grow, and the DVI cultures require a long lag time before they begin to acidify, it is unlikely that the thermophiles are actually delivering that much in most cases in terms of improved flavour or texture. For this reason I've suggested you use a homofermentative mesophilic culture but, should you choose to use a blend that includes some thermophiles too, keep the room warm during curd drainage to maximize their potential impact.

For a stronger flavour, more typical of the kinds of cheese being made in farmhouses across the Balkans, it is possible to add some lipase powder to the milk when the starters are added. Alternatively, using a rennet paste rather than rennet liquid to coagulate the curd, as is traditional practice, will have the same effect as adding lipase as the pastes contain pre-gastric esterase, an enzyme that hydrolyses fat. The lipase is optional if you are using rennet liquid, but should not be used alongside rennet paste.

YOU WILL NEED

11.4 litres/3 US gallons whole cow's, goat's or sheep's milk

1 unit R704 (Christian Hansen) or 0.7 DCU MA11 (Danisco) or equivalent homofermentative mesophilic starter

1.25ml/¼ tsp lipase powder (optional)

2.9ml/just over ½ tsp rennet liquid (or rennet paste) of 1:10,000 strength (see page 32)

8 per cent w/w brine – made up of 80g/3⅛oz salt per 1 litre/34fl oz water

salt

EQUIPMENT

Large stainless-steel pan; thermometer; spoon; pH meter; weighing scales; syringe or measuring tube; knife; ladle; tall cheese moulds or pond baskets; tray; lidded containers or a bowl

TIME

Coagulation time: 2–3 hours; drainage time: 15 hours; drying time: 24–48 hours; maturation time: 4–6 weeks

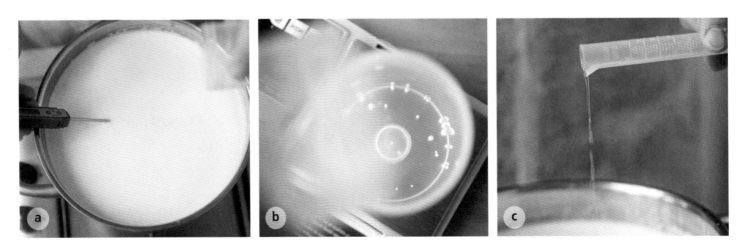

1 Pour the milk into the pan and gently heat it to 34°C/93°F, stirring continuously with a wooden spoon to prevent the milk from sticking on the base of the pan. Remove the pan from the heat when the milk gets to temperature and record its pH.

2 Weigh and add the starter culture (and lipase, if using) and stir into the milk. Leave to stand for 1 hour.

3 Measure the rennet liquid or paste with a syringe or measuring tube, then stir it in thoroughly for 1 minute. Leave the curd to coagulate for 50 minutes. The first signs of coagulation should be seen after about 20 minutes but the curd should be left for a further 30 minutes before it is cut.

4 Using a knife, make several parallel cuts spaced 2cm/¾in apart. Make a second series of cuts of the same spacing but at 90 degrees to the first.

5 Perform the final cuts by holding the knife at 45 degrees to the curd and making a series of diagonal cuts to reduce the columns down to rough cubes measuring about 2cm³/¾in³.

6 Leave the cut curd undisturbed for 10 minutes to allow the surface of the curd particles to 'heal', during which time a little whey is lost and the curd becomes slightly firmer.

7 Ladle the curd into tall cheese moulds or pond baskets, place them on a tray and leave them to drain for 3 hours. The cheeses will drain down to about a third to a quarter of their initial height.

8 Turn over the moulds and leave to drain for 12 hours in a warm room. ▶

g

h

i

j

9 After this time, check the pH of the drained curd; it should have reached about 4.80–4.60 by this time. Remove the cheeses from the moulds.

10 Sprinkle then rub dry salt on to the surface of each cheese to coat lightly, then leave them in a cool place, at around 15°C/59°C for 24–48 hours to dry.

11 Turn each of the cheeses once or twice during this drying time, rubbing a little more salt on to the surface of each when you do.

12 Transfer the cheeses to a lidded container or a bowl containing 8 per cent w/w brine. The volume of brine should be two or three times that of the cheeses. Cover the bowl, if using, with clear film or plastic wrap.

13 Place the container or bowl in the refrigerator for 4–6 weeks before use.

14 Once it is ready, lift out a block of cheese from the brine and slice off the required amount. The rest can be returned to the brine for further maturation.

Halloumi-style Cheese

An elastic, slightly squeaky texture and salty, umami flavour give this halloumi-style cheese a substantial, meaty quality. Serve it grilled, broiled or dry-fried until golden with a squeeze of lemon juice or a sprinkling of sumac for a snack or as part of a larger spread for a meal.

YOU WILL NEED

11.4 litres/3 US gallons whole sheep's, goat's, cow's or mixed milk

0.4 units STB-01 (Christian Hansen) STAM-3 (Danisco) or similar *Streptococcus thermophilus* thermophilic starter culture

3ml/⅗ tsp rennet of 1:10,000 strength (see page 32)

3–4 per cent w/w salt (35g/1½oz based on a predicted yield of 1kg/2¼lb

10ml/2 tsp dried mint

EQUIPMENT

2 large stainless-steel pans; thermometer; wooden or metal spoon; weighing scales; syringe or small measuring tube; knife; hand-held balloon whisk; sieve; cheesecloth; 2 chopping boards; weight; tray; cup; slotted spoon; small lidded container

TIME

Production time: about 2 hours; chilling time: 12 hours

1 Pour the milk into the pan and gently heat it to 34°C/93°F, stirring continuously with a wooden or metal spoon.

2 Weigh out and add the starter, if using pasteurized milk, and stir it in briefly.

3 Remove from the heat. Measure the rennet and stir for 1 minute, then leave for 45 minutes. The first signs of coagulation should be seen after 15 minutes, but leave the curd for 30 minutes more. ▶

Halloumi, a traditional product from the island of Cyprus and one of its major export products, is typically made with sheep's and goat's milk. A distinctive cheese, it appears in many recipes in the region, where its salty tang and firm texture lend flavour and substance to all manner of dishes.

The high scald temperature employed during the production of halloumi, with blocks of curd sitting in hot – almost boiling – whey for half an hour, exceeds the time and temperature required for pasteurization, with the result that this recipe is one of the safer cheeses to make with raw milk should you wish to do so.

For many of the other cheese recipes in this book, achieving successful acidification is the main concern. Halloumi is a little different – the aim here is to avoid significant acidification, keeping the pH of the fresh cheese at about 6.00. At this pH, curds do not melt and stretch particularly well and the cheese will brown when it is grilled, broiled or fried, retaining a satisfyingly squeaky texture.

Much is made of the fact that halloumi is produced without starter culture but it would be a mistake to assume that these traditional cheeses, or even the industrial ones, are sterile; thermoduric (heat-stable) lactic acid bacteria present in the raw milk as well as non-starter lactic acid bacteria (NSLAB) play an important role. Since the home dairy is unlikely to be a rich source of beneficial environmental contaminants and the microflora of raw milk that has been stored for any length of time is likely to be dominated by spoilage bacteria rather than natural lactic acid bacteria, it makes considerable sense for the home cheesemaker to add a tiny amount of starter culture – sufficient to reduce the pH slightly and provide some microbial competition in the early stages of the make but not enough to exceed the pH target significantly.

4 Cut the curd 45 minutes after renneting. Using a knife, make several parallel cuts spaced 2cm/¾in apart. Make a second series of cuts of the same spacing but at 90 degrees to the first.

5 To perform the final cut, start stirring gently with the balloon whisk, breaking the columns of curd down as evenly as is possible to around 1cm³/½in³ cubes.

6 Raise the temperature to 40°C/104°F over the course of about half an hour, stirring gently to keep the curds moving.

7 Check the temperature of the curds frequently during this time. They should start to firm up and, if the stirring is carried out carefully, the whey should remain a greenish-yellow colour. Do not discard the whey at this point – it will be used to scald the blocks of curd.

8 Cease stirring; the curd should sink to the bottom of the pan.

9 Line a sieve with cheesecloth, place it over a second pan and strain the curd and whey through it.

10 Gather up three corners of the cloth and tie the fourth one once around them in a 'Stilton knot' (see page 88).

11 Press the bag of curd between two boards with a weight placed on top and leave to drain in a tray for 30 minutes.

12 Meanwhile, prepare the whey. Heat the pan of whey up to 90°C/194°F. Whey proteins will rise to the surface, forming anari – a ricotta-type cheese that may be skimmed off, moulded and drained in much the same way (see pages 96–7). ▶

13 Once the curds have stopped rising, the whey is ready to use.

14 Rehydrate and sterilize the dried mint by steeping it in a cup of the hot whey for 5 minutes. Strain off the liquid and set aside the rehydrated mint.

15 Untie the Stilton knot and remove the cloth from the parcel of draining curd.

16 Using a sharp knife, cut the block into sections 2–3cm/¾–1¼in thick and immerse them in the hot whey for half an hour. The curd blocks should become firmer, taking on the texture of cooked chicken breast fillet and should rise to the surface of the whey.

17 Carefully remove the blocks from the whey using a slotted spoon.

18 Weigh the cheese and calculate how much salt is required, then rub this on the surfaces of the cheeses.

19 Sprinkle some of the reserved rehydrated mint on the face of the each cheese block, then fold them in half to secure the seam of mint running through the cores.

20 Transfer the cheeses to a small lidded container and leave them to cool in the refrigerator overnight. The halloumi can be enjoyed immediately or should be stored in the refrigerator in a lidded container and used within a week.

21 To prepare the halloumi for the table, slice the cheese perpendicular to the seam of mint and grill, broil or pan-fry it for 5–10 minutes, turning occasionally, until golden brown. Serve with some fresh lemon juice to squeeze over, if you like.

SOMETHING A BIT HARDER...

The hard and extra-hard cheeses require a little more time commitment both during cheesemaking and ripening, and the yield of curd is lower than that of the soft or fresh cheeses. Despite this, it is worth making your own for the reward of cutting into a ripened home-made Cheddar or Cheshire and discovering the delicious flavours that have been unlocked during the months of maturation.

While it follows a very similar process to Cheddar, the Caerphilly recipe produces a cheese that may be eaten at a few weeks old, and is a good introduction to the basic recipe used in the production of these British hard cheeses, without the extended ripening period. The Lancashire cheese-make is a little more involved, requiring curd from several consecutive days to be blended, though the complexity of flavour this produces repays the effort.

The hard cheeses of continental Europe can be elastic in texture and buttery and mild when young – such as Tomme – then becoming more complex as they age, with cheeses such as Gruyère and Gouda taking on a sweet, nutty taste and granular texture.

Provolone and Grana-style Cheese

The Italian style of hard-cheese technology has given us two different but related cheese types: the *pasta filata* or 'stretched-curd' cheeses, such as Provolone and Caciocavallo; and the Grana-style cheeses such as Grana Padano and Parmigiano Reggiano.

These cheeses are scalded to a high temperature so the dominant lactic acid bacteria are thermophilic – principally *Lactobacillus helveticus*. The use of natural whey starter (NWS) is traditional practice sometimes referred to as 'back slopping', and involves employing whey from one day's production as a starter for the next. While the cross-contamination risk may be viewed with some apprehension, in the case of these types of thermophilic cheese the processing steps of scalding the make at a high temperature and holding the whey at 50°C/122°F, when the pH falls below 4.00, control the growth of pathogens. The application of NWS is a little beyond the scope of most home cheesemaking operations, however, so here a thermophilic DVI culture is used.

Lipolysis plays an important role in the flavour development of these cheeses and, rather than liquid rennet extract, it is common for rennet paste to be used, with kid and lamb preparations providing stronger flavours than those obtained from calves. The paste contains a lipase enzyme, pre-gastric esterase. Should it not be available, substitute standard liquid rennet and add some lipase powder.

Grana-type cheeses are normally very large and the method can be difficult to adapt to a smaller scale. We shall therefore concentrate on the recipe for a *pasta filata* cheese that uses a similar process to the one used to make Provolone (shown left), and a modified grana-style cheese. For these, the curds are broken with a wooden spoon rather than being cut with a knife or the wooden stick called a *rotula* that was traditionally used.

YOU WILL NEED

11.4 litres/3 US gallons whole cow's milk

0.5 units STB-01 (Christian Hansen)
or TA50 (Danisco) or equivalent
thermophilic *Streptococcus
thermophilus* starter

0.5 units LHB-02 (Christian Hansen)
or LH100 (Danisco) thermophilic
Lactobacillus helveticus starter –
alternatively, there are several
starter blends available, such as
Su-Casa or TM 81 (Danisco)

3ml/⅝ tsp rennet (or rennet paste)
of 1:10,000 strength (or adjusted
accordingly, see page 32)

up to 1.25ml/¼ tsp lipase powder
(if not using rennet paste)

olive oil, for rubbing

EQUIPMENT

2 large stainless-steel pans, plus a lid;
thermometer; wooden spoon; pH
meter; weighing scales; syringe or
small measuring tube; slotted spoon;
measuring jug or cup; sharp knife;
heatproof bowl; loaf tin or pan; brine
tank (see page 39); cheesecloth;
unvarnished wooden board

TIME

Production time: 6 hours; brining time:
24 hours; maturation time: 1 month

PROVOLONE

1 Gently heat the milk in a pan to 37°C/
98°F, stirring occasionally with a wooden
spoon. Remove from the heat when it gets
to temperature and record its pH.

2 Measure and add the starter culture and
lipase (if not using rennet paste) and stir in
well. Leave for 1 hour, stirring occasionally.

3 Stir in the rennet for 1 minute, then
leave for 45 minutes. The first signs of
coagulation should be seen after about
15 minutes but the curd should be left to
firm up for 30 minutes more. Test the curd
before cutting (see pages 34–5).

4 Using the wooden spoon, stir and break
up the curds for 10 minutes, until they are
the size of rice grains. When the stirring
stops, the curds should sink rapidly to the
bottom of the pan.

5 Without disturbing the curd, pour off
the whey into the second pan and heat it
to 80°C/176°F, scooping off the ricotta
that surfaces (see page 97).

6 Measure the volume of the curds in a
measuring jug or cup, then return the
curds to the pan. Pour a volume of whey
into the pan. This should be roughly twice
as much as the volume of the curd, which
by now should have matted together into
a solid block.

7 Place a lid on the pan to retain the heat
and leave the block of curd steeping in the
hot whey for 1 hour.

8 Pour off the whey and test the pH of the
curd. The target for stretching is around
pH 5.20. If this has not been reached,
leave the curd in the pan covered with a
lid in a warm place to acidify further. ▶

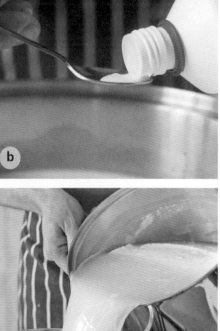

9 The acidification may take several hours and the curd temperature should be kept above 30°C/86°F. Record the pH periodically, pouring off any whey.

10 When the pH has reached 5.20, weigh the curd, then cut it into 1cm/½in-thick slices and put them in a heatproof bowl. Add 1 litre/34fl oz hot water at 95°C/203°F for every 1kg/2¼lb curd. Stir until the curd starts to melt into a single mass. It is normal for the water to look quite cloudy at this point.

11 Stretch and shape the curds into a single smooth-sided ball by folding the ball in on itself until the surface is smooth.

12 Shape the curd by putting it in a loaf tin or pan lined with cheesecloth to create a brick-shaped cheese. Turn over the block every 15 minutes as it cools, until it is able to hold its own shape outside the tin or pan. Alternatively, tear off pear-shaped pieces of curd – 400g/14oz each – then twist the narrow end to create a 'balloon-neck' that can later be used to string up the cheeses as they mature.

13 Transfer the cheese(s) to a brine tank (see page 39). Brine the 'bricks' for 24 hours and the 'pears' for 12–18 hours.

14 Remove the cheese(s) from the brining tank and dry for 24 hours at room temperature before coating with olive oil.

15 Mature the cheese(s) at around 20°C/68°F for at least a month, wiping them with oil every couple of weeks. The bricks should be matured on an unvarnished wooden board, while the pear-shaped cheeses can be strung up from a beam. They will continue to become firmer and more crystalline as they age.

GRANA-STYLE CHEESE

1 Using a 50:50 mixture of whole and skimmed milk, follow the Provolone-style cheese method up to step 3.

2 In step 4, cut the curd to the size of rice grains using a hand-held balloon whisk rather than a wooden spoon, stirring for 15–30 minutes while the temperature is raised rapidly to 55°C/131°F over a medium heat. When the curds are 'ready', they should appear reasonably firm and compact and sink rapidly to the bottom of the pan.

3 Remove the pan from the heat, cover with a lid and leave the curd to settle to the bottom of the pan for 1–1½ hours.

4 Carefully pour off the whey, gather the block of curd into a cheesecloth and place it in a hard-cheese mould. While the larger versions of these cheeses that are normally made are not pressed, this smaller size will need to be pressed gently using a 500g–1kg/1⅛–2¼lb weight.

5 Turn over the cheese in the mould once or twice; the pH should reach 5.40–5.00 within a few hours.

6 Place the cheese in a brine tank and leave it to brine for 24 hours.

7 Remove the cheese from the brining tank, then dry it at room temperature for up to 24 hours before rubbing the outside with some olive oil.

8 Mature the cheese on an unvarnished wooden board for 6–12 months at 20°C/68°F, turning it and wiping it with oil every 2 weeks, until it becomes hard and crystalline.

PARMIGIANO REGGIANO: A CONSIDERED APPROACH

Few cheese-production systems are as well thought out as that of Parmigiano Reggiano, which begins with evening milk being held overnight at ambient temperature, allowing the cream to separate and float to the surface, from where it is skimmed and churned into butter. While the feeding of silage to cows supplying milk for Parmigiano production is not permitted, the pH of the cheese means that it is at risk from late-blowing defect (see Troubleshooting on pages 198–9). However, as the separation of the cream overnight is likely to pull out a large proportion of bacteria and spores from the milk, including those of *Clostridium tyrobutyricum*, the procedure may help to limit the occurrence of late-blowing defect. It is probable that the reduction of the fat content of the milk makes the cheese less likely to go lipolytically rancid during the long maturation.

Once the cream has been skimmed off to be made into butter, a small quantity of whey is held back to be used as a starter for the following day's make; the remainder is fed to the pigs used in the production of Parma ham. Butter, cheese, charcuterie: a holistic approach to food production and the makings of a very good lunch.

Cheddar Cheese

Classic farmhouse Cheddar is mild and buttery when young, becoming harder and more intense as it ages, often with slightly sharp green-apple flavours or more brothy savoury notes. Larding and cloth-binding brings a pleasingly cellar-like quality to the aroma.

YOU WILL NEED

11.4 litres/3 US gallons whole cow's milk

1.5 units R704 (Christian Hansen), or 0.7 DCU RA21 or MA11 (Danisco) or equivalent predominantly homofermentative mesophilic starter

3ml/⅗ tsp rennet of 1:10,000 strength (or adjusted accordingly, see page 32)

2 per cent w/w salt (about 20g/¾oz based on a predicted yield of 1kg/2¼lb)

50g/2oz lard or butter, for greasing

EQUIPMENT

Large stainless-steel pan; thermometer; wooden spoon; pH meter; weighing scales; syringe or small measuring tube; hand-held balloon whisk; 1kg/2¼lb hard-cheese mould with follower; cheesecloth; 20 litre/5¼ US gallon lidded bucket or drum; sharp knife; small pan; cheese muslin; food-grade felt-tipped pen or a luggage tag; unvarnished wooden board; waxed paper

TIME

Production time: 5 hours; pressing time: 15–16 hours; maturation time: up to 6 months

Many cheeses lay claim to the title 'king of cheeses', but there are few recipes that have been embraced so universally as that of Cheddar, which originated in the area around the Somerset town in England from which it took its name. Cheddar was not always this popular, however; Gloucester and the almost-forgotten 'Wiltshire Loaf' seem to have been held in much higher regard 200 years ago. It was the ease with which Cheddar was adapted to large-scale production, as well as the modernizing influence of the 'father of Cheddar cheese', Joseph Harding, which helped tip the balance in favour of this now ubiquitous variety.

'Block cheddar', slabs of cheese matured in vacuum-packs, accounts for much of the worldwide production but there are still some exceptional farmhouse cheeses, smeared with lard and wrapped with cloth; the natural moulds on the rind carrying the aroma of the maturing room. While industrial Cheddar is more often made using direct vat inoculation (DVI) starters, traditional Cheddars are usually made with bulk starters that are prepared from frozen culture. These are not really suitable for home production for economical as well as practical reasons so the recipes in this book use DVI starter.

'Cheddaring' refers to the blocking and stacking of the curds to achieve the characteristic Cheddar texture; after the whey has been drained and the pile of curds has matted together, it is cut into sections that are piled one on top of the other to improve drainage. This recipe has been modified with regard to blocking and stacking – with a smaller quantity of curd, the block drains freely and stacking is not required to achieve the correct texture.

In this recipe, the curds are milled once they reach the target pH – though 'titratable acidity' is the preferred measure of acid production for traditional Cheddar-makers (see pH and Acidity on pages 36–7). A Cheddar mill is used by many producers, but it is quite a specialized piece of equipment and, given the small quantity of curd, the home cheesemaker would do better shredding it by hand.

The milled curds have an appearance often described as resembling 'chicken breast' – a satisfyingly accurate description. Few people can resist tasting the freshly milled and salted curds, which have a delightfully squeaky texture. Canadian students on my cheesemaking courses tend to become particularly excited by them, extolling the virtues of *poutine* – a dish of French fries, curds and gravy.

Cheddar requires approximately four times the weight used for pressing some of the continental hard cheese recipes. The home cheesemaker can replicate this by placing a water-filled lidded bucket or drum with a capacity of 20 litres/5¼ US gallons on top of the follower ('lid' of the mould).

The Red Leicester recipe makes an interesting variation on the Cheddar one. It is coloured with annatto, a liquid extract made from the seeds of a South American shrub *Bixa orellana*. This is used to add a pleasing orange colour to several cheese types, including coloured Cheddar and Cheshire, Red Leicester and Shropshire blue, as well as enhancing the rind colouration of some washed-rind cheeses, such as Livarot. ▶

1 Gently heat the milk in the pan to 32°C/90°F, stirring occasionally with a wooden spoon. Remove from the heat when it gets to temperature and record its pH.

2 Weigh and stir in the starter culture. Leave for 1 hour, stirring occasionally to incorporate any cream that surfaces.

3 Measure the rennet, then stir in for 1 minute then leave to stand for 45 minutes. The first signs of coagulation should be seen after 15 minutes, but the curd should be left for 30 minutes more before cutting.

4 Test the curd before cutting (see pages 34–5). Using a hand-held balloon whisk and a gentle stirring motion, cut the curd to cubes of about 5mm³/¼in³ over about 5 minutes, then leave it undisturbed to heal for 5 minutes more.

5 Stir the curd every 5 minutes for 1 hour in total, gradually raising the temperature (scalding) to 40°C/104°F in approximately 2°C/3.6°F increments. By the end of the hour, the curds will have shrunk, becoming firm and compact pellets and taking on an appearance often described as 'shotty'.

6 When the scald is complete, stop stirring and allow the curd to sink below the greenish-yellow whey for 5 minutes.

7 Pour off the whey, being careful not to lose any of the curds. Record the pH at this point – it should have dropped to around 6.30–6.20.

8 Push the curds to one half of the pan and prop up the curd side so that any whey drains off to the opposite side of the pan. Leave like this for 15 minutes; the curds will knit together into a block.

9 After 15 minutes, turn over the block, test the pH of the whey and pour it off. Prop up one side of the pan to encourage the whey to drain away from the curd.

10 Continue to turn over the block of curd every 15 minutes, recording the pH each time. On average, the pH should drop around 0.15 every 15 minutes. Once the pH reaches 5.45–5.40, the curd is ready for milling. This target is normally reached in a little over 1 hour.

11 Weigh the curd, then measure out 2 per cent of the cheese's weight in salt. To calculate this, divide the weight of the curd in grams by 100 and then multiply the result by 2.

12 Shred or mill the curd by hand into rough chunks measuring 2.5 × 5cm/1 x 2in. The shredded curd should resemble cooked chicken and it is not unusual to feel strangely hungry at this point – but patience now will be well rewarded later...

13 Sprinkle half of the salt by hand over the curds, mixing until they are evenly coated. Wait for 5 minutes, then add the remaining salt, mixing well.

14 Leave the curds for about 15 minutes to 'mellow', during which time the salt draws out any excess moisture from the curd. At this point it is acceptable to succumb to hunger and have a little taste – it is delicious! ▶

RED LEICESTER

Leicester cheese roughly follows the production process for Cheddar, but 1.25ml/¼ tsp annatto is stirred in with the starter. Follow the Cheddar process but cut the curd very finely with the whisk – 'until it is almost the appearance of coarse sand,' explained Dora Saker in *Practical Dairying* (1921). Scald the grains to 37°C/99°F and, after blocking and turning, the curd is milled when the pH reaches 5.50–5.45 and should be ground up finely before pressing or, if being used, pass the curd through a peg mill twice. The cheese is ready after 6–8 weeks.

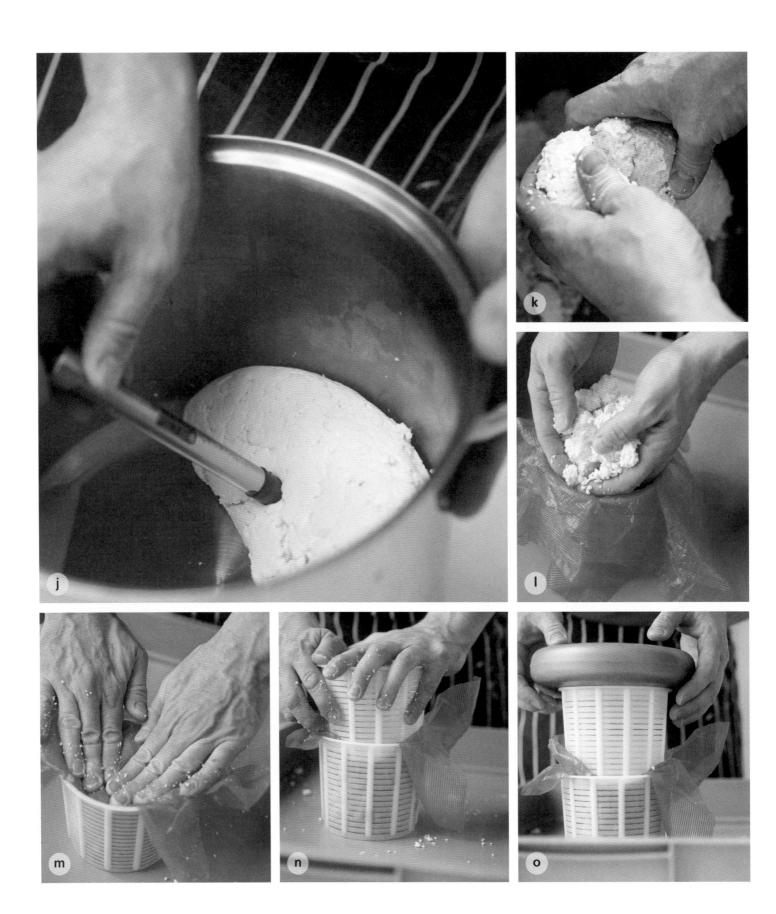

15 The temperature of the curd prior to pressing should be about 22°C/72°F. Higher temperatures may result in an excessive loss of fat while lower ones may result in curds that do not fuse together adequately, so it needs to be correct.

16 Pack the curds into a hard-cheese mould lined with cheesecloth and press for 1–2 hours with the lidded bucket or drum only a quarter full of water.

17 Remove the cheese from the press and turn it over in the mould, pulling the cloth taut as you do so to remove creases. Place the follower on the cheese. Completely fill the lidded bucket or drum with water and stand it on the follower to press the cheese for about 12 hours.

18 Remove the cheese from the press, turn it out of the mould and remove the cloth. Using a sharp knife, trim off any untidy scraps of curd to neaten the edges.

19 Melt the lard, or butter if this is not available, in the small pan. Cut two discs of cheese muslin a little wider than the diameter of the cheese and a rectangular strip wide and long enough to go once around the cheese with a slight overlap.

20 Soak the muslin in the liquid fat, then smooth the top and bottom pieces in place before wrapping the strip round the side. As the fat cools, the material should adhere to the surface of the cheese. Return the cheese to the mould and press it for several hours while this happens.

21 Mark the date of production on the cheese either using a food-grade felt-tipped pen directly on to the cloth or by stitching on a luggage tag on which the date is written. ▶

p

q

22 Mature the cheese on an unvarnished wooden board in a cool larder or the refrigerator at about 12–15°C/53–59°F for 5–6 months; smaller cheeses mature faster than the usual 23kg/50lb farmhouse Cheddar truckles, which are aged for more than 9 months. Turn the cheese each week and brush down the natural moulds that will appear on the surface.

23 Once unwrapped and sliced, wrap the Cheddar cheese in waxed paper and store it in the refrigerator. Bring it to room temperature before eating it.

DUNLOP

Following the improvements Joseph Harding made to the recipe, Dunlop was undoubtedly much changed from the cheese that Barbara Gilmour is claimed to have invented in the 17th century. Dunlop today refers to a mild, buttery Cheddar-style cheese. To make Dunlop, follow the Cheddar recipe but scald the curd to just 36°C/97°F and, following blocking and turning, mill the curd when it reaches pH 5.20.

Cheshire Cheese

Not a melting cheese, the moist, crumbly texture and salty, savoury flavour of Cheshire means
that is is best enjoyed simply, perhaps with some crusty bread and an apple or some crunchy
celery sticks, without any need for further accompaniments.

Cheshire, like many of the traditional cheeses hailing from the north of England, is crumbly in style. This recipe follows a similar process to that of the more-elastic Cheddar but with some subtle differences relating to the drainage and acidification.

Calcium retention is essential for cheeses for which a high degree of elasticity is required. This is because slow drainage or fast acidification tend to cause more calcium to be lost from the curds, which become brittle as a result.

When Cheddar is made, the curd is cut quite finely and later blocked and stacked to improve whey drainage. For Cheshire, a higher dose of starter is used, the curds are not cut so finely, and instead of being blocked and stacked, they are broken up to enhance the crumbly character of the finished cheese.

There is some argument about whether coloured or uncoloured Cheshire is the most traditional; either way, there are certainly references to the use of annatto, the orange dye from the *Bixa orellana* shrub, in the historical cheesemaking texts that are held at the British Library. The acidity of Cheshire bleaches the cheese, resulting in a paler colour than the golden-yellow of Cheddar. In Britain 200 years ago, pale cheese was taken to be a sign of inferior quality in the markets of London, so the addition of a small amount of annatto to lend that all-important colour would certainly have helped to dispel such prejudice and seems fairly likely. Both coloured and uncoloured versions of Cheshire are made today and both can be delicious.

YOU WILL NEED

11.4 litres/3 US gallons whole cow's milk

1.8 units R704 (Christian Hansen) or 0.9 DCU RA21 or MA11 (Danisco) or equivalent mesophilic starter

3ml/⅗ tsp rennet of 1:10,000 strength (or adjusted accordingly, see page 32)

2 per cent w/w salt (20g/¾oz based on a predicted yield of 1kg/2¼lb)

50g/2oz lard or butter, for greasing

EQUIPMENT

Large stainless-steel pan; thermometer; wooden spoon; pH meter; weighing scales; syringe or small measuring tube; sharp knife; 1kg/2¼lb hard-cheese mould with follower; cheesecloth; 3–4kg/6.6–8.8lb weight or a 20 litre/5¼ US gallon lidded bucket or drum; pan; cheese muslin; food-grade pen or a luggage tag; unvarnished wooden board; waxed paper

TIME

Production time: 5 hours; pressing time: 38 hours; maturation time: 1–2 months

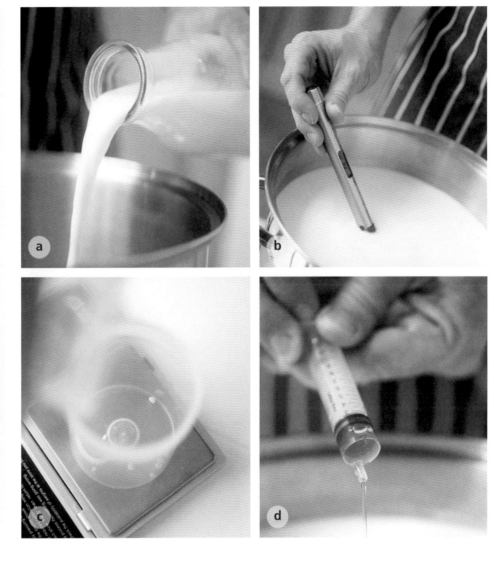

1 Pour the milk into the pan and gently bring it to 33°C/91°F, stirring occasionally. Remove from the heat when it gets to temperature and record the pH of the milk.

2 Weigh the starter culture, then add it to the milk and stir it in well. Leave for 1 hour, stirring occasionally to incorporate any cream that has risen to the surface.

3 Measure the rennet then stir it in for 1 minute. Leave for 45–50 minutes. The first signs of coagulation should be seen after 15–20 minutes but the curd should be left for a further 30 minutes before cutting.

4 Test the curd (see pages 34–5) before cutting it. Using the knife, make a series of even parallel cuts spaced 1cm/½in apart, then turn the pan through 90 degrees and make a second series of crossways cuts with the same spacing.

5 For the final cut, hold the knife at 45 degrees to the curd and make a series of diagonal cuts. Leave to heal for 5 minutes.

6 Stir the curd every 5 minutes over the course of 45 minutes, maintaining a temperature of 33°C/91°F. If it drops below this, return the pan to a low heat.

7 Stop stirring and allow the curd to sink below the greenish-yellow whey and leave it for 5 minutes.

8 Pour off the whey, being careful not to lose any of the curds. Record the pH of the curds at this point – it should have dropped to about 6.00.

9 Push the curds to one half of the pan and prop up the curd side so that any whey drains off to the opposite side of the pan. Leave the pan positioned in this way for about 15 minutes, during which time the curds will knit together. ▶

10 Test the pH of the whey that has collected in the pan and pour it off. Write down the pH as this reading will be used for comparison purposes to assess the acidification in 15 minutes' time.

11 Tear up the curds roughly by hand and prop up one side of the pan again to encourage the whey to drain away.

12 Continue to record the pH about every 15 minutes, pouring off the whey and breaking up the curd. On average, the pH should drop 0.15–0.20 every 15 minutes.

13 Once the pH reaches 5.20, the curd is ready for milling. This target pH is normally reached in 1 hour. Weigh the curd, then measure out 2 per cent of the cheese's weight in salt. To calculate this, divide the weight of the curd in grams by 100 and then multiply the result by 2.

14 Crumble the curd into rice-sized grains by hand and mix in half of the salt, also by hand, until the curds are evenly coated. Using your hands enables you to ensure even distrubution. Wait for 5 minutes then add the remaining salt, mixing it in well.

15 Leave the curds for 15 minutes to 'mellow', during which time the salt draws excess moisture from the curd.

16 The temperature of the curd prior to pressing should be about 22°C/72°F. Higher ones may result in an excessive loss of fat while lower ones may result in curds that do not adequately fuse together.

17 Pack the curds into a hard-cheese mould lined with cheesecloth and press for 1–2 hours with the weight or the lidded bucket or drum filled with water.

18 Unmould the cheese and replace it in the mould upside down, pulling the cloth taut and covering the cheese. Replace the weight, drum or bucket and press the cheese overnight.

19 Remove the cheese from the press, turn it out of the mould and remove the cloth. Trim off any untidy scraps of curd to neaten the edges.

20 In the pan, heat the lard, or butter if this is not available, until it melts.

21 Cut two discs of cheese muslin a little wider than the diameter of the cheese and a rectangular strip that is wide and long enough to go once around the cheese with a slight overlap. ▶

COLOURED CHESHIRE
Add 1.25ml/¼ tsp annatto to the milk with the starter culture and stir in well. The recipe then proceeds as for uncoloured Cheshire.

22 Soak the muslin in the molten lard or butter and then smooth the top and bottom pieces on to the large surfaces of the cheese before wrapping the strip around the side. As the fat cools, the material should adhere to the surface of the cheese.

23 Return the cheese to the press for another 24 hours while the material sticks to the cheese.

24 Mark the date of production on the cheese either using a food-grade felt-tipped pen and writing directly on to the cloth or by stitching on a luggage tag on which the date is written.

25 Mature the cheese on an unvarnished wooden board in a cool larder or the refrigerator at about 12–15°C/53–59°F for 1–2 months, turning it weekly and brushing off any natural moulds that may appear on the surface.

26 Once unwrapped and sliced, wrap the cheese in waxed paper and store it in the refrigerator. Bring the cheese to room temperature before eating it.

Caerphilly

Bearing some similarities to the Cheddar recipe but being aged for a fraction of the time, Caerphilly is crumblier and more lactic in flavour. The cheese is unusual in that it is both dry-salted and brined and it is then ready to eat in about 2 weeks.

The 1934 edition of *The Ministry of Agriculture and Fisheries Bulletin 43*, a guidance document issued for the instruction of farmhouse cheesemakers, reminds its readers that Caerphilly is a cheese associated with the mining districts of Wales and the South West of England. There could be several reasons for its popularity in these mining communities. Some writers maintain that it would have been a good way of replacing salt lost during hard physical labour, but there is perhaps an even simpler explanation: Caerphilly is a fast-maturing cheese that is easier to produce than Cheddar, and therefore likely to have been a cheap, accessible food for the regions' working-class families. Many producers still make cheese using traditional methods (see the Gorwydd Caerphilly, below) and this recipe will enable you to achieve similar results.

YOU WILL NEED

11.4 litres/3 US gallons whole cow's milk

1.5 units R704 (Christian Hansen), or 0.7 DCU RA21 or MA11 (Danisco) or equivalent predominantly homofermentative mesophilic starter

3ml/⅗ tsp rennet of 1:10,000 strength (or adjusted accordingly, see page 32)

1 per cent w/w salt (12g/½oz based on a predicted yield of 1.2kg/2½lb)

EQUIPMENT

Large stainless-steel pan; thermometer; wooden spoon; pH meter; weighing scales; syringe or small measuring tube; knife; 1.2kg/2½lb hard-cheese mould with follower; cheesecloth; 20 litre/5¼ US gallon lidded bucket or drum; brine tank (see page 39); unvarnished wooden board; waxed paper

TIME

Production time: up to 6 hours; pressing time: 12–13 hours; brining time: 6 hours; drying time: 24 hours; maturation time: 2 weeks

1 Gently heat the milk in the stainless-steel pan to 32°C/90°F, stirring occasionally with a wooden spoon. Remove from the heat when up to temperature and record its pH.

2 Weigh the starter culture then stir it in well. Leave for 1½–2 hours, stirring occasionally to incorporate any cream that has risen to the surface.

3 Measure the rennet, then stir it in well for 1 minute before leaving the curd to coagulate for 35–40 minutes. The first signs of coagulation should be seen after 15–20 minutes but the curd should be left to firm up for a further 20 minutes before cutting.

4 Test the curd (see pages 34–5) before cutting it. Using the knife, make a series of even parallel cuts spaced 1cm/½in apart, then turn the pan through 90 degrees and make a second series of crossways cuts with the same spacing.

5 For the final cut, hold the knife at 45 degrees to the curd and make a series of diagonal cuts. Leave to heal for 5 minutes.

6 Return the pan to the heat and stir the curd continuously with a spoon for 30 minutes, gradually raising the temperature to 34°C/93°F. During this time the curds will lose moisture and shrink slightly, firming up as they do so.

7 Stop stirring and allow the curd to sink below the whey. Leave the curds under the whey until the pH drops to 6.20. Pour off the whey, being careful not to lose any of the curds.

8 Push the curds with a spoon to one half of the pan and prop up this curd side so that any whey drains to the opposite side of the pan.

9 When the pH reaches 6.00, discard the whey that has collected and slice the curd into 2cm/¾in strips, piling them loosely on one side of the pan.

10 When the curd reaches pH 5.60, weigh the curd and chop it with a knife into 2cm³/¾in³ cubes. ►

11 Measure out 1 per cent of the cheese's weight in salt. To calculate this, divide the weight of the curd in grams by 100. Evenly sprinkle the salt over the curd and gently mix it in.

12 The temperature of the curd prior to pressing should be about 22°C/72°F. Higher ones may result in an excessive loss of fat while lower ones may result in curds that do not adequately fuse together.

13 Line the hard-cheese mould with cheesecloth, then pack in the curds. Put on the follower and weight it with the lidded bucket or drum a quarter full of water. Press the curds for 30 minutes.

14 Remove the cheese from the press and turn it in the mould, pulling the cloth taut as you do so. Half-fill the drum or bucket with water and press the cheese for 12 hours.

15 Remove the cheese from the press, turn it out of the mould and remove the cloth. Trim off any untidy scraps of curd with a knife to neaten the edges. Transfer the cheese to a prepared brine tank and leave it for 6 hours.

16 Remove the cheese from the brine tank and leave it to drip-dry for 24 hours.

17 Mature the cheese on an unvarnished wooden board in a cool larder or the refrigerator at about 12–15°C/53–59°F for at least 2 weeks, turning every 2 days. The surface may develop some natural moulds as it ages further.

18 Once it has been unwrapped and sliced, wrap the cheese in waxed paper and store it in the refrigerator. Bring it to room temperature before eating it.

Lancashire

This is a crumbly, buttery and mild cheese that nonetheless shows incredible depth of flavour. The make is a little more complex than some but the end result repays the effort and the cheese is ready to eat after only a few months.

FOR EACH DAY'S CURD, YOU WILL NEED

7.6 litres/2 US gallons whole cow's milk

0.7 units Flora Danica or 0.6 units CHN-11 (Christian Hansen), or equivalent heterofermentative mesophilic starter culture

2.3ml/scant ½ tsp rennet of 1:10,000 strength (or adjusted accordingly, see page 32)

50g/2oz lard or butter, for greasing

WHEN THE CURDS ARE MIXED, YOU WILL NEED

2 per cent w/w salt (about 50g/2oz for a 2-day curd or 70g/2¾oz for a 3-day curd)

EQUIPMENT

Large stainless-steel pan, thermometer; wooden spoon; pH meter; weighing scales; syringe or small measuring tube; knife; draining tray; cheesecloth; 2 lidded plastic containers; curd mill or mincer (optional); large bowl or tray; 2–3kg/ 4½–6¾lb hard-cheese mould; 20 litre/ 5¼ US gallon lidded bucket or drum; small pan; cheese muslin; unvarnished wooden board; waxed paper

TIME

Production time: about 6 hours each day for 2–3 days; pressing time: 18 hours; maturation time: 2 months

Some producers of Lancashire cheese blend curd from two different days, whereas industrially manufactured cheeses may only contain sharp and acidic curd from 1 day. Perhaps the best-tasting cheese, however, is made using the 3-day curd method, which blends three curds with differing acidities.

The process of the blending of curds from different days most likely came about for practical reasons. The milk yield from small herds, or even a few cows on a smallholding, wouldn't be sufficient in just 1 day to create the curds required to make a large cheese, so it would have to have been collected over several days. This approach can be taken by the home cheesemaker, too, giving them an opportunity to make a fairly substantial cheese over 2–3 days.

There are a few other examples of mixed-curd cheeses in Europe, such as Bleu de Termignon and Tarentaise, and I have taught this kind of methodology on professional courses at the School of Artisan Food. The thing that really stands out for me is that when tasting curd from several days, the flavour of the blended curd is always greater than the sum of its parts.

Lancashire is sold as 'creamy' when it has been aged for more than 2 months and 'tasty' when it has been aged for more than 5 months. To my palate, neither is especially strong-flavoured if made well, the cheese delivering complexity and depth rather than assertiveness.

1 Gently heat the milk in the pan to 30°C/ 86°F, stirring occasionally with a wooden spoon. Remove from the heat when the milk gets to temperature and record its pH.

2 Weigh and then add the starter culture and stir in well. Leave for 1 hour, stirring occasionally to incorporate any cream that has risen to the surface. ▶

3 Measure the rennet, stir it in well for 1 minute, then leave the curd to stand for 50–55 minutes. The first signs of coagulation should be seen after about 10–15 minutes but the curd should be left to firm up for a further 40 minutes before it is cut.

4 Test the curd (see pages 34–5) before cutting it. Using the knife, make a series of even parallel cuts spaced 1cm/½in apart, then turn the pan through 90 degrees and make a second series of crossways cuts with the same spacing.

5 For the final cut, hold the knife at 45 degrees to the curd and make a series of diagonal cuts. Leave to heal for 5 minutes.

6 Stir the curd briefly with a spoon for 5 minutes, then allow it to sink to the bottom of the pan and leave it to stand for 45 minutes.

7 Pour off the whey through a draining tray lined with cheesecloth to collect the curds. Gather the corners of the cloth and press the curd briefly but gently by hand to squeeze out a little more retained whey.

8 Leave the curds in the cloth in the tray and leave to drain for 15 minutes.

9 Tip the curds into the tray and break up roughly by hand. Leave it to drain again for 20–30 minutes. Repeat this process three or four times, by which point the curd should be well drained and the pH should be 6.00 or above.

10 Transfer the curd to a plastic container, put on the lid and leave it at room temperature (about 20°C/68°F), until the following day.

11 On day 2, repeat steps 1–9. If you are making a 2-day curd cheese, proceed to step 13.

12 If you are making a 3-day curd, store the curd from day 2 in a lidded plastic container at room temperature (about 20°C/68°F), and repeat steps 1–9 on day 3.

13 On the final day, weigh and taste each of the batches of curd. The older curds should taste fairly sour, while the young ones should taste sweet. Record the pH of each batch, then blend them together.

14 Chop the combined curds finely with a knife, then pass them through a curd mill three times or pass them through a well-sterilized mincer. Alternatively, you can use your hands. The curds should be ground very finely to resemble shredded suet or chilled, grated shortening.

15 Measure out 2 per cent of the curds' weight in salt. To calculate this, combine the weight of the curds from each day in grams, divide the total by 100 and multiply it by 2 to give the weight of salt required in grams.

16 In a large bowl or tray, combine the curds with the measured salt and mix it together thoroughly over 5 minutes to ensure it is completely combined.

17 Pack the curds into a cheese mould lined with cheesecloth and leave to stand for 6 hours for the curd to consolidate, without pressing.

18 Turn the cheese in the mould, pulling the cloth taut, then press for at least 6 hours more, weighted with the drum or bucket half-filled with water. ▶

19 Remove the cheese from the press, turn it out of the mould and remove the cloth. Trim off any untidy scraps of curd to neaten the edges.

20 In the small pan, heat the lard, or butter if this is not available, until it melts. Cut two discs of cheese muslin a little wider than the diameter of the cheese and a rectangular strip that is wide and long enough to go once around the cheese with a slight overlap.

21 Soak the muslin in the molten lard or butter and then smooth the top and bottom pieces on to the surfaces of the cheese before wrapping the strip around the side. As the fat cools, the cheese muslin should adhere to the surface of the cheese.

22 Fill the drum or bucket completely with water and return the cheese to the press in the mould for about 6 hours.

23 Mature the cheese on an unvarnished wooden board in a cool larder or the refrigerator at about 12–15°C/53–59°F for at least 2 months, turning it every week and brushing down any moulds that appear on the rind.

24 Once it has been unwrapped and sliced, wrap the cheese in waxed paper and store it in the refrigerator. Bring it to room temperature before eating it.

Gouda

Mild and buttery when young but taking on an intense toffee sweetness as it ages, this cheese pairs well with good ham, crusty bread and strong, slightly sweet coffee. It is well worth making yourself; the difference between good Gouda and mass-produced cheese is striking.

YOU WILL NEED

11.4 litres/3 US gallons whole cow's milk
0.8 units CHN-11 or Flora Danica (Christian Hansen) or Kazu (Danisco) or equivalent heterofermentative mesophilic starter
2.9ml/generous ½ tsp rennet of 1:10,000 strength (or adjusted accordingly, see page 32)
plastic cheese-coating (such as Plasticoat®)

EQUIPMENT

Large stainless-steel pan; thermometer; wooden spoon; pH meter; syringe or small measuring tube; hand-held balloon whisk; ladle; hard-cheese mould; cheesecloth; 1kg/2¼lb and 2kg/4½lb weights; brine tank (see page 39); unvarnished wooden board; waxed paper

TIME

Production time: 4 hours; pressing time: 24 hours; brining time: 6–12 hours; drying time: several hours; maturation time: 2–12 months

AGED GOUDA

The finished cheese may be matured in a cool larder at about 10–15°C/ 50–59°F on an unvarnished wooden board for a further 8 months, during which time it will lose moisture and become more crystalline, acquiring a rich caramel flavour.

Correctly pronounced 'how-da', the Dutch town from which this cheese hails is famed for two foods, which are celebrated in the architecture of two of its municipal buildings: one is criss-crossed in lines which make it look like a *stroopwafel* (syrup waffle); the other is wide and flat, has a few large, round windows and bears a similarity to the cheese that has made the town's name famous worldwide.

Developed by a sea-going nation with a colonial heritage, it should not be surprising that Gouda is found pretty much everywhere, but it is a pity that it has become synonymous with a lot of rather bland, young and rubbery offerings in the supermarket. Good Dutch farmhouse cheese – *Boorenkaas* – is exceptional, with the best examples often staying in the Netherlands.

A visit to a Dutch cheese shop is quite an experience, the counter spilling over with piles of exquisitely arranged Goudas of every possible age and with many variations: *Oude Gouda*, aged and crystalline like Parmesan with complex caramel flavours; *Jonge Kaas*, young and buttery; *Brandnetel Kaas*, a 'flavour-added' version made with dried stinging nettles; and *Nagelkaas* ('nail cheese') made with cloves. There are also some excellent goat's milk versions.

Gouda is a washed-curd cheese, which means that during the stirring of the curd some of the whey is drained off and replaced with warm water. This rinses lactose from the curds before the starter bacteria can turn it into lactic acid, which keeps the pH relatively high. The paste is a golden-yellow colour and the slow pH development during drainage ensures that the cheese retains a high degree of elasticity. Gouda that ends up being inelastic, pale or crumbly is likely to have acidified too quickly or drained too slowly.

Because of their high pH, another common problem frequently found in these cheeses is late-blowing defect, excessive gas production in the paste due to the spore-forming bacteria *Clostridium tyrobutyricum* (See Troubleshooting on pages 198–9). Late-blowing defect is associated with feeding silage to the milking herd. It is inhibited commercially by the addition of a small amount of lysozyme to the milk, an enzyme derived from egg white that inhibits *Clostridium*. However, this enzyme may be hard for the home cheesemaker to source it so it might make sense to produce Gouda only during the summer when the amount of silage being fed to dairy cows is likely to be lower.

The presence of the right kinds of lactic acid bacteria is crucial to achieving the cheese's characteristic flavour development. In addition to *Lactococcus lactis* subsp. *lactis* and *L. lactis* subsp. *cremoris*, starters also include aromatic strains such as *L. lactis* subsp. *lactis biovar diacetylactis* and *Leuconostoc mesenteroides*, which help to impart a rich, buttery flavour. These aromatic strains are never used on their own but are added at a ratio of 10–30 per cent to homofermentative strains, either as a ready-mixed DVI, such as Flora Danica, or as a combination of an acidifying culture and an aromatic culture.

1 Pour the milk into the large pan and gently warm it to 32°C/90°F, stirring occasionally with a wooden spoon. Remove from the heat when the milk gets to temperature and record its pH.

2 Weigh and then add the starter culture and stir in well for 1 minute. Leave the starter to rehydrate for 1 hour.

3 Measure the rennet and stir it in well for 1 minute.

4 Leave the curd to coagulate for about 40 minutes. The first signs of coagulation should be seen after about 20 minutes but the curd should be left to firm up for a further 20 minutes before it is cut. Test the curd is ready before you start cutting (see pages 34–5).

5 Using the balloon whisk in a gentle stirring motion, begin to cut the curd into cubes measuring 5mm³–1cm³/¼–½in³ over a period of 5 minutes.

6 Stir the curd with the spoon, briskly but gently, for about 10 minutes. The whey should be green-yellow in colour rather than white. The latter colour indicates damage has been caused to the curd by over-enthusiastic stirring.

7 Stop stirring, allow the curd to settle to the bottom of the pan and gently pour off 3.78 litres/1 US gallon of the whey. Replace it with an equal volume of water at 46–50°C/115–122°F. ▶

8 Stir the curds in the water and whey mixture for 5 minutes. The addition of the warm water should bring the temperature of the curd to 36–38°C/97–100°F.

9 Stop stirring and allow the curds to sink to the bottom of the pan. Measure and record the pH of the whey; it should not have changed much, if at all, since the start of the make.

10 Pour off most of the liquid from the pan until the remaining whey just covers the curds.

11 At this stage it is very important to press the curds together under the surface of the whey to minimize air pockets within the paste of the cheese. To do so, keeping as much of the curd submerged as possible, gather it into a pile that is roughly the same diameter as the cheese mould and gently press it down by hand to help it to knit together.

12 Once the curd has matted, transfer it to the mould and press it immediately. The cheese should be subjected to a weight that is about three times that of the cheese. A 1kg/2¼lb cheese will require 3kg/6¾lb of weight to be placed on the follower, but it is important to add the weight gradually, adding only 1–2kg/ 2¼–4½lb immediately after moulding.

13 After 2 hours of being pressed, remove the cheese from the mould, turn it over and replace it into the mould so that it is upside down.

14 Measure and record the pH of the curd. Replace the weights on the cheese mould, adding the additional weight so that three times the weight of the cheese is applied in total.

15 Press the cheese for several hours, until no further whey drains off, by which point the pH should have reached at least 5.40 but not be lower than 5.00.

16 Remove from the mould and place the cheese in a brine tank for 6–12 hours for a 1–2kg/2¼–4½lb cheese, increasing this time by 24 hours or more for a larger one. Turn it in the brine about every 3 hours.

17 Remove the cheese from the brine and leave it to drip-dry for several hours before painting the plastic cheese-coating on the top and sides using a scrap of cheesecloth.

18 Allow the cheese to dry for several hours before turning it over and repeating the process on the other side. Repeat again on each side after 1 week.

19 Mature the cheese on an unvarnished wooden board in a cool larder at about 10–15°C/50–59°F. Turn it every day for the first week, then every week thereafter. Wipe it with a clean, damp cloth periodically to inhibit surface moulds.

20 Once sliced, wrap the cheese in waxed paper and store it in the refrigerator. Bring it to room temperature before eating it.

FLAVOURED GOUDA

Made with various herb mixes, flavoured Goudas are usually eaten young – at about 2 months old. Boil the herbs for a few minutes in a little water and allow them to cool for an hour before adding them to the curds in step 8. Stir well before pressing and moulding the curd. Some common flavourings include: fenugreek, cumin, mustard seeds or chilli flakes.

Gruyère

This cheese has sweet and nutty flavours and an elastic, yielding texture in youth, becoming harder and sometimes slightly crystalline and developing layers of complex flavour as it ages. It is a perfect match with potato-based dishes and is the cheese classically associated with fondue.

YOU WILL NEED

11.4 litres/3 US gallons whole cow's milk

1 unit MY800 or ALP D (Danisco),
  0.05 dose Thermo C (Biena) or
  equivalent thermophilic starter

0.3ml/¹⁄₁₆ tsp *Propionibacterium
  freudenreichii* subsp. *shermani*

2.9ml/generous ½ tsp rennet of
  1:10,000 strength (or adjusted
  accordingly, see page 32)

1.5 per cent w/w salt, 15g/½oz based
  on a predicted yield of 1kg/2/¼lb

For the *morge* (ripening culture)

15ml/3 tsp salt

500ml/17fl oz water

Either: 0.02 dose PLA ripening culture
  (Danisco)

Or: 0.01 dose *Geotrichum candidum*
  (Geo 17 from Danisco), plus

0.01 dose *Debaryomyces hansenii*
  (DH from Danisco), plus

0.01 dose *Brevibacterium linens*
  (BL1 from Christian Hansen or
  SR1 from Danisco)

(the PLA culture includes the above
  strains plus *Arthrobacter nicotinae*)

EQUIPMENT

Large stainless-steel pan; thermometer; wooden spoon; pH meter; weighing scales; syringe or small measuring tube; hand-held balloon whisk; wide cheesecloth or sheet; hard-cheese mould; tray; weights; unvarnished board of pine, spruce or larch; plastic container wide enough to fit around the cheese; waxed paper

TIME

Production time: 2 hours; pressing time: 6 hours; salting time: 24 hours; maturation time: 4 months

High in the Alps, in remote chalets and sometimes still with beautiful copper vats, cheesemakers practise a form of production that has been carried out almost unchanged for hundreds of years, taking their herds high into the mountains to feed on the Alpine pasture, making cheese through the summer then returning to the valley for the winter – and possibly more lucrative work as ski instructors!

The name Gruyère is given to an AOP cheese produced in the valley of that name in Switzerland but there are cheeses produced by the same kind of technology elsewhere, including two very well-known examples from France: Beaufort from the Rhône-Apes region and Comté from Franche-Comté, the latter of which makes up the greatest volume of cheese produced in France.

These cheeses are characterized by their sweet and nutty flavours and by rinds that are typically washed, or smear-ripened, during their maturation. Some of these cheeses are very large; sometimes using about 500 litre/110 US gallons of milk to make a single 40kg/88lb cheese.

In the commercial production of many of these cheeses, a thermophilic whey starter is used; the whey from the previous day's production being held at a high temperature overnight and mixed with some slices of dried calf abomasum (the fourth stomach from which rennet enzyme is obtained) to create a starter-and-coagulant 'in one' solution. For the home cheesemaker, the starter should include *Streptococcus thermophilus* and *Lactobacillus delbrueckii* subsp. *bulgaricus* and *Lactobacillus helveticus*, but some starter blends also incorporate mesophilic strains. The thermophiles will remain dominant though, given a competitive advantage by the high scald temperature.

The make itself is a very rapid process with the cheeses often being formed in little over an hour. The coagulation time is short, the curd is cut very finely to the size of rice grains or smaller, and a high scald temperature is used to encourage whey drainage. There are considerable similarities between this and the Gouda recipe in that the curds are gathered together under the whey. In this case, a cloth is passed underneath the curds as they settle on the base of the vat, then lifted out and placed in a mould that is quickly transferred to the press.

Like Gouda, the pH remains high, typically at about 5.30, and the cheeses are just as prone to late-blowing defect (see Troubleshooting on pages 198–9). The feeding of silage to the herd is not permitted in the AOC rules for many of these types of cheese. The home cheesemaker is unlikely to have much say in the feeding of the cows and they may do well to follow the example of the Alpine cheesemakers, making cheese only in the summer when it is likely that less silage is used.

The characteristic flavours of these cheeses are influenced by propionic acid bacteria such as *Propionibacterium freudenreichii* subsp. *shermani*; a ripening culture that ferments lactic acid into propionic and acetic acids. It also produces carbon dioxide, which is responsible for the large, round holes, or 'eyes' in Emmental and similar cheeses. These bacteria are not particularly salt tolerant and their growth is encouraged by the low levels of salt in these cheeses. In the case of Emmental, this may be 1 per cent or less, resulting in the formation of large eyes.

This cheese is an introduction to some of the smear-ripened soft cheeses that we will explore later in the book, the surface of the cheese being washed for several weeks with *morge* – a ripening culture of yeasts and bacteria. ▶

1 Pour the milk into the pan and warm it to 34°C/93°F, stirring occasionally with a wooden spoon. Remove from the heat and measure and record the pH.

2 Weigh and measure the starter and ripening cultures then add to the milk and stir in well for 1 minute. Leave for 1 hour.

3 Stir in the rennet for 1 minute, then leave to stand for 30 minutes. The first signs of coagulation should be seen after 20 minutes but the curd should be left to harden for 10 minutes more before it is cut.

4 Using the balloon whisk in a brisk figure-of-eight motion, begin to cut the delicate curds 30 minutes after the addition of the rennet. The curds should be cut down to the size of rice grains.

5 Begin to heat the pan, scalding the curds by raising the temperature of the whey to 50°C/122°F steadily over a period of 30 minutes. Stir the curd with the whisk continuously throughout the scalding process – by the end of the time the curds should resemble tiny specks and the whey will be greenish-yellow.

6 Remove from the heat and stop stirring. The curd should sink instantly.

7 Slide the cheesecloth underneath the curd, which should have started matting at the bottom of the pan, capturing as much of it as possible. Take care as the whey will be hot; work quickly or wear plastic gloves.

8 Gather together the four corners of the cheesecloth and lift the whole mass out of the whey. Squeeze the cloth to release whey and swiftly transfer the curds and cloth to the mould.

9 Weigh the curds, then place the mould in a tray to catch the whey that will be pressed out. Press the curds immediately using a weight that is about three or four times that of the cheese.

10 Leave these cheese in a warm room for a total of about 6 hours. After 2 hours, remove the cheese from the mould, peel back the cloth, turn over the cheese and wrap it again neatly.

11 Return the cheese to the mould, then replace it under the weights on the press. Record the pH and continue to monitor it until the pH reaches 5.40–5.20 – this will take about 4 hours more.

12 After this time, remove the cheese from the mould and place it on an unvarnished board of pine, spruce or larch. The temperature during the early ripening should be about 20°C/68°F, which may be best achieved by ambient storage.

13 Rub half of the salt into the surface of the cheese. Place an upturned plastic container over the cheese to maintain the humidity level. Leave for 12 hours. ▶

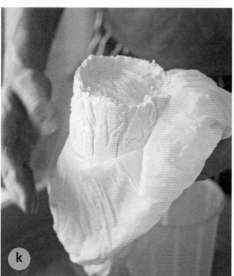

14 Turn over the cheese and rub in the remainder of the salt. Leave for 12 hours.

15 Prepare the *morge* by combining the salt, water, yeasts and bacteria. Turn the cheese and rub some of the *morge* into the top and sides using cheesecloth or your fingers. Replace the container.

16 Turn and wash the cheese with *morge* every day for a week. The surface should become matt and slimy as the yeast and smear bacteria begin to grow, then start to develop a pink-orange pigmentation.

17 Once the smear is well developed, stop washing the surface with the *morge*. Instead, the cheese should now be turned once a week and wiped with some dry cheesecloth. The smear should gradually darken, taking on a brownish hue while the cheeses are matured for at least 2 and up to 4 months, during which time the temperature may be dropped to 10–15°C/50–59°F.

18 Once sliced, store the cheese in waxed paper in the refrigerator, but bring it to room temperature before eating.

EMMENTAL

The Emmental recipe follows the same process but using 0.6ml/⅛ tsp of *Propionibacterium freudenreichii* subsp. *shermani*. Emmental is usually brined but it may be difficult to moderate the salt level in a very small cheese so a home cheesemaker should dry-salt the rind at 0.8 per cent w/w rather than the 1.5 per cent used in the Gruyère recipe. This is about 8g/¼oz based on a predicted yield of 1kg/2¼lb. Maturation should follow the same process.

Tomme

This cheese with its slightly elastic paste shows a sweet, floral and buttery flavour that is a pleasing counterpoint to the mildly musty, soil-like aroma that rises from the rind, which is covered in patted-down filaments of white or grey mould.

Tomme is a fairly generic word that has been applied to many different types of cheese, but in its most common usage it defines the fairly elastic styles made in the Alps, but perhaps most famously in the Savoie region of France. These are typically quite small, weighing about 1.6kg/3½lb or less, and while there are many examples of tomme made in large creameries, its origins are rooted in the lofty farmhouses of the Savoie. These are cheeses that could be produced when milk supplies were limited at the start and end of the milking season or that could be made from the skimmed milk left after butter-making, matured briefly and consumed in the farmhouse.

Even today, some *fermier* cheesemakers produce tomme for a few days after returning to the high-Alpine pasture before they commence production of their 'premium' cheeses, preparing the microflora of the dairy. Others produce tomme over the winter months from the handful of animals that might still be in milk; the milk from any species may be used, though cow's milk is most common.

Tomme has a natural mould rind typically dominated by species of *Penicillium* or *Mucor*. The latter might concern a soft cheesemaker but on tomme it is desirable and should not be discouraged. The cheeses should start to grow short white hairs, which darken as they grow, taking on a silver-grey appearance best described by the French '*poil de chat*' (cat's fur). After the moulds have taken hold, the surfaces of the cheese are brushed to pat them down and the rind takes on its typical grey-brown appearance.

YOU WILL NEED

11.4 litres/3 US gallons whole cow's milk, or 50:50 semi-skimmed and whole milk

0.5 unit STB-01 (Christian Hansen) or MY800 (Danisco) or equivalent *thermophilic Streptococcus thermophilus* or yogurt starter

0.5 unit Flora Danica (Christian Hansen) or equivalent heterofermentative mesophilic starter

3ml/⅗ tsp rennet of 1:10,000 strength (or adjusted accordingly, see page 32)

1.5 per cent w/w salt (about 15g/ generous ½oz based on a predicted yield about 1kg/2¼lb)

EQUIPMENT

Large stainless-steel pan; thermometer; wooden or metal spoon; pH meter; weighing scales; syringe or small measuring tube; hand-held balloon whisk; hard-cheese mould; cheesecloth; ladle; weights; brine tank (see page 39) (optional); unvarnished board of pine, spruce or larch; plastic container wide enough to fit over the cheese

TIME

Production time: 1¾ hours; pressing time: about 8 hours; brining time; 4–6 hours (optional); maturation time: 1–2 months

1 Pour the milk into the pan and warm it to 33°C/91°F, stirring occasionally with a spoon. Remove from the heat, then measure and record the milk's pH.

2 Weigh then add the starter culture, stirring it in well before leaving it to rehydrate for 30 minutes.

3 Measure the rennet and stir it in for 1 minute before leaving it for 35 minutes. The first signs of coagulation should be seen in about 15 minutes but the curd should be left for a further 20 minutes.

4 Cut the curds using the balloon whisk in a gentle figure-of-eight motion for 5 minutes. The size should be somewhere between corn grains and hazelnuts.

5 Begin to heat the pan, scalding the curds by steadily raising the temperature of the whey to 40°C/104°F over the course of 30 minutes, stirring constantly with the wooden or metal spoon. Since the curds are quite delicate after cutting, stirring should be extremely gentle at first, becoming a little more vigorous as they lose whey and sink to the bottom of the pan more readily. ▶

a

b

c

d

e

f

g

h

6 Once the target temperature is reached, stop stirring and remove the pan from the heat. The curds should begin to sink to the bottom of the greenish-yellow whey, most of which can be poured off, leaving enough to just cover the curds.

7 Test and then record the pH of the curds – at this point it should not have changed significantly since the start of the make and is likely to be above 6.40.

8 Line the hard-cheese mould with cheesecloth, then ladle in the curds or scoop them using the mould.

9 Press the curds immediately with a weight equal to that of the finished cheese. There should be enough curd to yield a single cheese with a final weight of about 1kg/2¼lb or two smaller cheeses weighing 500g/1⅛lb a piece. Leave to press in a warm room.

10 After about 2 hours' pressing, remove the cheese from the mould and carefully peel back the cheesecloth.

11 Turn it over and wrap it more neatly in the cloth before returning it to the mould, making sure that the side that was on the bottom during the first press is now at the top.

12 Record the pH of the curds and replace the weight. Press the cheese overnight or for about 6 hours, until the pH reaches 5.00–5.40.

13 Carefully remove the cheese from the mould and cheesecloth and rub the salt into the rind. Alternatively, it is possible to brine the cheese for 4–6 hours, depending on its size. (See Salting and Brining on pages 38–9.) ▶

THE ALPINE PASTURE

There is something quite special about the cheeses made by transhumant farmers in the Alps. These cheeses reflect a way of life practised over hundreds, if not thousands, of years, but it is one that is being challenged. It takes someone quite extraordinary to want to live on the side of a mountain for 5 months each year with limited connectivity to the outside world and with only 20 cows for company!

High above the treeline, as the snows recede – as late as June or July – the mountains become covered in a dazzling array of Alpine flowers, sent out from tenacious plants growing low to the ground. With every 5–10m/5–10yds walked, the composition of the mountain flora can change dramatically and it is this diversity of pasture on which the cows graze that influences the incredible taste of the milk and the cheeses made from it.

14 Place the tomme on an unvarnished board and mature it at about 10°C/50°F initially to encourage the growth of natural moulds. Cover with an upturned plastic container to maintain high humidity. The moulds will be patchy when they first appear. When there is a good amount of silvery-grey mould, mature the cheese in cooler conditions – 8–12°C/47–53°C – and gently brush or pat down the moulds when turning the cheese on a weekly basis. Mature for at least 1 month and up to 2 months. Turn the cheese every week.

15 Once sliced, store the cheese in waxed paper in the refrigerator, but bring it to room temperature before eating.

SAINT NECTAIRE-STYLE CHEESE

From the Auvergne region of France, Saint Nectaire is best described as being a 'mixed-rind' cheese with a natural mould rind that is also washed to encourage flavour development.

Use whole cow's milk and follow the tomme recipe, but cut the curd to the size of wheat grains. After stirring, scalding and moulding, press the cheese with twice its own weight. Unmould and salt the cheese, then place it on wooden boards and mature it at 8–9°C/47–48°F. After 1–2 days, wash the rind in 3 per cent salt solution. Repeat twice a week for 2 weeks, after which moulds should grow on the rind.

MANCHEGO-STYLE CHEESE

To make an approximation of a manchego (shown right), follow the tomme recipe using sheep's milk and a coagulation time of 30 minutes. Cut the curds a little finer than you do for tomme, as the high fat content of the sheep's milk can impede the drainage of the whey. When the cheeses are unmoulded, rub the rinds (which will be thinner than those of commercial manchego) with olive oil weekly to discourage mould growth and dispense with the plastic container. Mature at 15–20°C/59–68°F. All of the other production processes stay the same.

SURFACE-RIPENED & BLUE CHEESES

These mould- and bacterially-ripened soft and semi-hard cheeses can be tricky recipes to get right, since the moisture content of the curd must be balanced perfectly to avoid flavour and texture defects, while the ripening requires carefully controlled humidity and temperatures to encourage the growth of the right kind of ripening organisms. The recipes in this chapter are, therefore, suitable for more ambitious or experienced home cheesemakers.

Blue cheeses include the Stilton-style Cheese, with its long, slow drainage, as well as slightly softer, more continental-European styles, all of which require salt, moisture and acidity levels to be exactly right. The Brie or Camembert recipe can be particularly challenging, requiring a delicate balance of yeasts and mould to provide flavour without bitterness.

We will also explore the recipes for a ripened version of the lactic curd cheese, with its surface yeasts and moulds, and two cheeses whose rinds are washed with brine (and sometimes alcohol) to encourage the growth of the sticky orange smear-bacteria that gives them their pungent aromas.

Stilton-style Cheese

One of the most famous blue cheeses in the world, Stilton is renowned for its its rich, fruity aroma, slightly crumbly texture, buttery mouthfeel and complex flavour. This recipe produces something a little different from modern commercial cheeses, and draws upon traditional techniques.

The traditional blue cheeses of Britain tend towards the firm or semi-hard rather than soft and the process by which they are made – milling and dry-salting acidified curds – bears a similarity to that used in the production of hard cheeses, such as Cheddar. As we saw during the blocking and stacking of the Cheddar's curd, it is important for the home cheesemaker to understand the objective of the process and not merely copy large-scale production techniques in miniature; sometimes what is done out of necessity when working with a thousand litres of milk is irrelevant when we are working with ten.

The way that Stilton is made has changed somewhat in the 80 years since the Ministry of Agriculture and Fisheries first published *Bulletin No. 43*, a guidance booklet for farmhouse cheesemakers that included a recipe for this famous blue cheese. There is no farmhouse Stilton produced in the UK today, the move towards larger-scale production having already begun 20 years before the publication of *Bulletin No. 43*. Nowadays, large vats of milk are coagulated, cut and ladled on to cloth-lined cooling tables, where they drain slowly overnight. Drainage progresses at a noticeably faster pace when the recipe is downscaled – producing an altogether different cheese.

To make a product at home that really starts to express some of the characteristics of one of the traditional British blue cheeses, we should forget about their modern-day equivalents and instead draw inspiration from the farmhouse recipes of a previous century when blue cheeses were made by ladling curds into cloth parcels, tying them with a Stilton knot and draining them in a 'sink', which can be plugged and unplugged periodically to slow the drainage as required.

As ever when making cheese, all of the equipment must be cleaned and disinfected because this cheese in particular can pose a high risk for *Listeria* and other pathogens.

1 Pour the milk into one of the pans and warm it to 29–30°C/84–86°F, stirring occasionally. Remove the pan from the heat when the milk gets to temperature and record the pH of the milk.

2 Weigh and add the starter culture, ripening yeasts and mould and stir in well. Put a lid on the pan to retain heat and leave the starter to rehydrate for 1 hour.

3 Measure and add the rennet and stir it in well for 1 minute before leaving the curd to coagulate for 1 hour. The first signs of coagulation should be seen 10 minutes after the addition of the rennet but the curd should be left to harden for a further 50 minutes before cutting.

4 In the meantime, line the second stainless-steel pan neatly with a square of finely-woven cotton sheet, pressing it down into the corners.

YOU WILL NEED
11.4 litres/3 US gallons whole cow's milk
0.7 units Flora Danica (Christian Hansen) or equivalent heterofermentative mesophilic starter
0.02 dose DH (Danisco) or equivalent *Debaryomyces hansenii* yeast
0.02 dose KL71 (Danisco) or equivalent *Kluyveromyces lactis* yeast
0.02 dose GEO17 (Danisco) or equivalent *Geotrichum candidum* yeast
0.02 dose PRB6 or PJ (Danisco) or equivalent *Penicillium roqueforti* ripening moulds, rehydrated in water

0.02 dose BL1 (Christian Hansen) or SR1 (Danisco) or equivalent *Brevibacterium linens* ripening bacteria (optional)
3.5ml/scant ¾ tsp rennet of 1:10,000 strength (or adjusted accordingly, see page 32)
2.3 per cent w/w salt

EQUIPMENT
2 large stainless-steel pans, plus a lid; thermometer; wooden spoon; pH meter; weighing scales; syringe or small measuring tube; 2 finely-woven cotton sheets wide enough to line the sides and

base of each pan; knife; ladle; tray; section of plastic pipe 12cm/4½in in diameter and 24cm/9in tall, or a home-made cheese mould of similar proportions (see page 19); cheesecloth; 2 plastic boards a little wider than the cheese moulds; draining table; blunt, round-ended knife; plastic draining mesh; plastic container or bucket; round stainless-steel skewer; waxed paper

TIME
Production time: 7 hours; hastening time: 3–7 days; maturation time: 9–10 weeks

5 Test the curd 60 minutes after renneting (see pages 34–5). It should appear quite firm. Make three equally spaced vertical cuts in the curd in one direction, then turn the pan 90 degrees and make three more. Leave the curd to heal for 15 minutes.

6 Using the ladle and being careful to damage the curd as little as possible, ladle it all into the cloth-lined pan. This should take no more than about 5 minutes. Do not attempt to squeeze the curds by gathering up the cloth at this stage.

7 Measure and record the pH. Discard any whey that is left after ladling out the curd, then wash the pan – you will need to use it again later.

8 After 1 hour, gather up the corners of the cloth and transfer the bundle quickly back to the first pan, aiming to avoid excessive whey-loss from the contained curds but leaving behind the whey that had already drained into the pan. It should be sitting in a pool of whey – do not try to squeeze out more whey than has drained off naturally.

9 Discard the whey that is left in the second pan, then wash the pan so it is ready for further use.

10 Measure and record the pH – it should be above 6.40 at this stage. Should it be lower than this, speed up the drainage by gathering the four corners of the bag and tying them in a Stilton knot (see page 88).

11 After another 1 hour, transfer the curd back to the second pan in the same way. The volume of the curd bundle should shrink with each transfer as more whey is lost, but the drainage process should not be hurried. ▶

12 Record the pH – it should be about 6.30 at this stage. Should it be lower than this, speed up the drainage by tying or retying the Stilton knot. If acidification is very fast, drainage may be slowed by releasing the knot and delaying the frequency of the transferral of the curd from pan to pan.

13 When the pH is approaching 6.00, tip the curd out of the cloth into one of the empty pans and cover it with a lid to keep it warm. The curd should be well drained by this point so the transfer of curd from pan to pan can stop.

14 Continue to check the pH every hour until the curd reaches 5.10–5.00. This could take several hours or even longer in a cold room, so keep the ambient temperature at about 25°C/77°F.

15 Weigh the curd, then tip it into a tray and break it up carefully into walnut-sized pieces by hand.

16 Measure out 2.3 per cent of the curd's weight in salt. To calculate this, multiply the weight of the curd in grams by 0.023 to give the quantity of salt needed.

17 Mix the salt into the cheese curds, being careful not to break them up into small pieces while at the same time ensuring that the salt is evenly distributed. Leave the curds for 15 minutes for some of the salt to be absorbed and a little whey to leak out.

18 Prepare the plastic pipe or cheese mould by lining it with cheesecloth. If you are using a tubular mould, position it upright on a plastic board. The cheese is likely to release some whey over the next few days, so it would be sensible to stand the board in the tray in which you broke up the curd or on a draining table, to collect the drips.

19 Pile the curds into the prepared mould. They should not be packed down or subjected to any weight or pressure as the openness of the curds is required to aid the growth of the blue moulds.

20 Place the second board on top of the mould and drape a dampened cheesecloth over the top to enclose it. Transfer the cheese, boards and all, to a room heated to 16–18°C/ 62–64°F for 'hastening', which will encourage drainage and the growth of the yeasts.

21 Turn over the cheese after 1 hour without removing the cheese from the mould, holding the boards firmly in place as the turn is made.

22 Leave the cheese in the mould at 16–18°C/ 62–64°F for several days or up to a maximum of 1 week, turning and covering it with a fresh dampened cheesecloth each day, until the sides of the cheese appear slightly slimy and smell yeasty and sweet.

23 Turn out the cheese from the mould after hastening is complete and scrape the sides gently with a blunt, round-ended knife to smooth over any splits or holes in the rind.

24 Place the cheese on a board lined with plastic draining mesh, cover it with the plastic container or bucket and transfer it to a larder or refrigerator at 12–15°C/54–59°F.

25 After 12 hours, scrape the sides of the cheese a second and final time and turn it over once before returning it to mature at 12–15°C/ 54–59°F, covered with the plastic container or bucket to retain humidity.

26 Turn over the cheese each day, gently wiping down the rinds with a clean scrap of cheesecloth. Stop wiping the cheese after the rind has formed, to allow it to become slightly dry and develop the characteristic crust. ▶

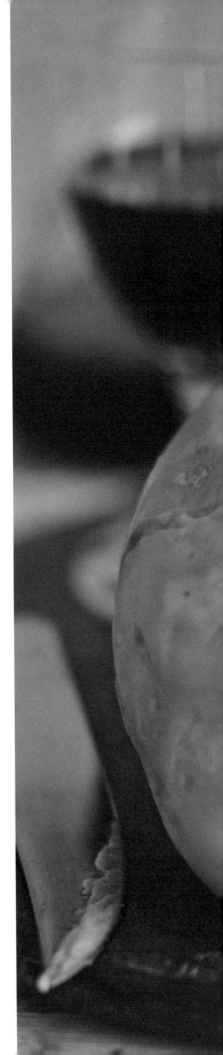

(m)

27 After 5 weeks, pierce the cheese with a sterilized round stainless-steel skewer, pushing the skewer halfway into the cheese. This should be done in about 20 places, evenly distributed over the rind of the cheese. After piercing, turn the cheese every other day.

28 Wrap the cheese in waxed paper and mature for at least another 4 weeks at 12–15°C/54–59°F, turning it every other day. The cheese can be matured for longer, with the flavour becoming stronger over time. Enjoy at room temperature and re-wrap in the waxed paper to store.

SKIMMED-MILK BLUE CHEESE
Dorset's Blue Vinney was granted a Protected Geographical Indication (PGI) in 1998. It is a strong blue cheese with dark-blue veins and was traditionally made from hand-skimmed milk. To reduce the fat percentage of the cheese to 1.5–1.8 per cent, rather than using whole milk, use semi-skimmed milk or a mixture of three parts whole milk to two parts skimmed milk.

SHROPSHIRE BLUE
To make a coloured variation of the Stilton recipe, shown right, add 1.2ml/ ¼ tsp annatto to the milk with the starter cultures and follow the recipe as stated.

Gorgonzola-style Cheese

This mountain-style cheese is slightly different from the rich, blue commercial Gorgonzola, and has a slightly dough-like aroma, a silky-soft texture as it matures and often minimal blueing. It is perfect served with crusty bread and charcuterie or can be used in a Béchamel sauce.

Gorgonzola, the traditional cheese of the Piedmont and Lombardy regions in the north of Italy can be a difficult technology to adapt to home production. Using thermophilic starters at the lowest limit of their growth temperature and produced in 10kg/22lb wheels, this is not a cheese that lends itself well to the domestic kitchen.

Instead, here we will make a mountain-style blue cheese using a two-curd method, variants of which have been practised in farmhouses in the Alpine regions for hundreds of years. Essentially the technique involves draining overnight the curds made on one day and mixing them with fresh curds from the following day's make. James Long and John Benson described such a method for making Gorgonzola in *Cheese and Cheese Making, Butter and Milk, With Special Reference to Continental Fancy Cheeses* (1896) and there are similar varieties made even today around the Col de Mont Cenis – the high Alpine pass between France and Italy.

There are two styles of Gorgonzola in modern production: the rich and creamy dolce style and the slightly firmer and stronger picante. This recipe is closer to the latter but offers something quite different to one made using the modern production process.

As ever when making cheese, all of the equipment used should be cleaned and especially carefully disinfected before use because this cheese in particular can pose a high risk for *Listeria* and other pathogens.

FOR EACH DAY'S MAKE, YOU WILL NEED
11.4 litres/3 gallons whole cow's milk
0.3 units STB-01 (Christian Hansen) or equivalent *S. thermophilus* thermophilic starter
0.7 units Flora Danica (Christian Hansen) or equivalent heterofermentative mesophilic starter
0.02 dose DH (Danisco) or equivalent *Debaryomyces hansenii* yeast
0.02 dose GEO17 (Danisco) or equivalent *Geotrichum candidum* yeast
0.02 dose PA (Danisco) or equivalent *Penicillium roqueforti* ripening moulds, rehydrated in some water
up to 1.25ml/¼ tsp lipase powder (optional)

2.9ml/just over ½ tsp rennet of 1:10,000 strength (or adjusted, see page 32)
coarse or flaked salt

EQUIPMENT
Large stainless-steel pan with a lid; thermometer; wooden spoon; pH meter; weighing scales; syringe or small measuring tube; knife; 3 cheesecloths; tray; plastic pipe 15cm/6in in diameter and 30cm/12in high, or a home-made cheese mould of similar proportions (see page 19); unvarnished wooden board; plastic draining mat; plastic container; round stainless-steel skewer; waxed paper

TIME
Production time: 6 hours over 36 hours; maturation time: 2–3 months

1 Pour the milk into the pan and warm it to 32°C/90°F, stirring occasionally with a wooden spoon to prevent it from sticking. Remove the pan from the heat when the milk gets to temperature and measure and record the pH of the milk.

2 Measure and then add the starter culture, lipase and ripening yeasts and moulds to the milk and stir in well to combine thoroughly. Put a lid on the pan to retain the heat and leave the starter to rehydrate for 1 hour.

3 Measure and add the rennet and stir it in well for 1 minute before leaving the curd to coagulate for 50 minutes. The first signs of coagulation should be seen 20 minutes after the addition of the rennet but the curd should be left to harden for a further 30 minutes before cutting.

4 Test the curd 50 minutes after renneting (see pages 34–5). It should appear quite soft. Using the knife, make a series of parallel cuts spaced 2cm/¾in apart, then turn the pan 90 degrees and make a second series of cuts with the same spacing.

5 For the final cut, hold the knife at 45 degrees to the curd and make a series of diagonal cuts. Leave the curd to heal for 15 minutes.

6 Gently stir the curd with a spoon for 1 minute every 5 minutes over a total of 45 minutes, during which time the surface of the curds should start to firm up.

7 Spread out a cheesecloth in the tray, then pour in the curds. Gather up the ends of the cheesecloth and knot them.

8 Hang the curd in a warm room at 20°C/68°F to drain and acidify overnight or for 12 hours. By the end of this time, the pH of the curd should have acidified to about 5.00 and will feel firmer and drier.

9 Repeat steps 1–7 to make another batch of curd. Hang up the new curd in a warm room at 20°C/68°F and allow it to drain for 30 minutes.

10 Use the knife to mince the curds from both batches into corn-sized grains.

11 Combine both batches of milled curd well and put them into a plastic pipe or a home-made cheese mould lined with a fresh cheesecloth. Leave at 20°C/68°F for 24 hours, turning over the cheese twice in the mould during this time, pulling the cloth taut each time to help to seal the rind. No weights are used for making this cheese. At the end of this time the pH of the curd should be about 5.00. ▶

12 Remove the mould and cheesecloth and turn the cheese out on to a wooden board lined with a plastic drainage mat. Rub a handful of salt into the cheese's rind.

13 Mature the cheese for 1 week at 20°C/68°F, turning it and rubbing another handful of salt into its rind each day.

14 Place it on the board in a room at 12°C/54°F and cover it with an upturned plastic container to retain humidity. Turn it every other day. Brush or wipe the rind weekly to inhibit surface-mould development.

15 After 4 weeks, pierce the cheese from top to bottom with a sterilized stainless-steel skewer at five to ten evenly distributed points. Piercing is not always practised when making cheeses of this type. This stage can be omitted if you prefer, although the cheese may be less blue and take longer to develop.

16 Wrap the cheese in waxed paper and leave it to mature for at least 3 weeks more at 12°C/54°F, turning it every other day. The cheese can be matured longer, with the flavour becoming stronger over time.

Fourme-style and Roquefort-style Cheeses

These cheeses are made in the same way as Gorgonzola-style ones, just with different types of milk. They have a moist, slighty crumbly paste that becomes smoother and more broken-down as the cheeses age. Old ends of the cheeses may be crumbled into salads to add intensity.

The blue cheeses of the Auvergne region of France are legendary: Fourme d'Ambert and Bleu d'Auvergne made from cow's milk, and Roquefort made from sheep's milk – specifically that of the Lacaune breed. The trick to getting these cheeses right is to use a gas-producing lactic acid bacteria called *Leuconostoc*, which creates the holes required for mould-growth. Unlike Stilton, this is not a cheese streaked with veins but instead one that presents neat pockets of mould growth on its cut face.

For Roquefort, the AOC rules permit only the use of *Penicillium roqueforti* cultured from traditional strains naturally present in the cellars of the region. Traditionally, loaves of rye bread are left to go mouldy, then crumbled to a powder that is scattered on to the layers of curd as they are placed in the moulds. The natural *Penicillium* in this case is typically green rather than blue. The striking difference between the paste and the moulds can be enhanced by the use of chlorophyll as a contrast dye, making the white look whiter and the green look greener.

This recipe uses several types of yeast and the requisite *P. roqueforti* ripening mould, and can be made with cow's milk to produce Fourme-style cheese or sheep's milk to create Roquefort-style cheese.

YOU WILL NEED
11.4 litres/3 gallons whole cow's or sheep's milk
0.7 units Flora Danica (Christian Hansen) or equivalent heterofermentative mesophilic starter
0.02 dose DH (Danisco) or equivalent *Debaryomyces hansenii* yeast
0.02 dose KL71 (Danisco) or equivalent *Kluyveromyces lactis* yeast
0.02 dose PRB6 or PJ (Danisco) or equivalent *Penicillium roqueforti* ripening moulds, rehydrated in a little water
up to 1.25ml/¼ tsp lipase powder (optional)
2.9ml/just over ½ tsp rennet of 1:10,000 strength (or adjusted, see page 32) if using cow's milk, or 1.45ml/just over ¼ tsp if using sheep's milk
coarse or flaked salt

EQUIPMENT
Large stainless-steel pan, plus a lid; thermometer; wooden spoon; weighing scales; pH meter; syringe or measuring tube; knife; plastic strainer; ladle; section of plastic pipe 10cm/4in in diameter and 20cm/8in tall, or a home-made cheese mould of similar proportions (see page 19); cheesecloth; tray; unvarnished wooden board; plastic draining mat; round stainless-steel skewer; laminated foil (not catering foil, which will corrode) or clear film (plastic wrap)
NB: All equipment should be cleaned and disinfected before use. These types of cheese can pose a high risk for *Listeria* and other pathogens.

TIME
Production time: 5 hours over 38 hours; maturation time: 2–3 months

1 Pour the milk into the pan and warm it to 30°C/86°F, stirring occasionally with a spoon. Remove from the heat when it gets to temperature and record its pH.

2 Measure and add the starter culture, lipase, ripening yeasts and mould and stir in. Put a lid on the pan to retain heat and leave the starter to rehydrate for 1 hour.

3 Measure and add the rennet and stir it in well for 1 minute before leaving it to coagulate for 2 hours. The first signs of coagulation should be seen 20 minutes after the addition of the rennet but the curd should be left to harden for a further 1 hour 40 minutes before cutting.

4 Test the curd 2 hours after renneting (see pages 34–5). It should be very firm. Using the knife, make a series of parallel cuts spaced 2cm/¾in apart, then turn the pan 90 degrees and make a second series of cuts with the same spacing.

5 For the final cut, hold the knife at 45 degrees and make a series of diagonal cuts. Leave the curd to heal for 15 minutes.

6 Gently stir the curd with a spoon for 2 minutes, then let it rest for 8 minutes. Repeat every 10 minutes over the course of 1 hour, during which time the surface of the curds should firm up. The curds should remain separate and free-floating; stir more often if they start to mat together.

7 After 1 hour, carefully drain the whey down to the level of the curd.

8 Stir once more, then scoop out the curds with a small plastic strainer, allowing most of the whey to drain.

9 Line the pipe or home-made cheese mould with cheesecloth and position it in a tray to catch the whey that drains, then ladle in the curds.

10 Leave the curd to drain for a total of 36 hours, turning the cheese after 2 hours and then another four times during the drainage time. The pH should drop below 5.00 by the end of this time. ▶

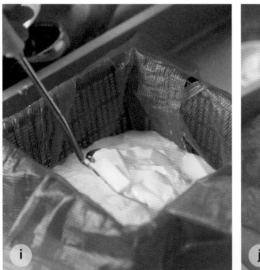

11 Carefully unmould the cheese and turn it out on to a board lined with a plastic draining mat.

12 Rub a small handful of coarse or flaked salt into the top, sides and bottom of the cheese until it is evenly coated in a fine layer of salt.

13 After salting, store the cheese at 10°C/50°F. Turn the cheese once on each of the following 2 days and repeat the salting each time, then leave it to mature, turning it every other day.

14 After 1–2 weeks, tightly wrap the cheese in laminated foil or clear film or plastic wrap and continue to mature it at 10°C/50°F, turning it every other day.

15 After 3 weeks, remove the wrapping and pierce the cheese on the top and bottom in five to eight evenly spaced points on each side using a sterilized stainless-steel skewer.

16 Wash the outside of the cheese in cold water and re-wrap it in a fresh piece of foil or clear film/plastic wrap.

17 Continue to mature the cheese at 10°C/50°F, turning it every other day for another 4 weeks.

18 Four weeks after piercing, wash the surface of the cheese in cold water to remove surface moulds – Roquefort-style cheeses should not have a rind.

19 Cut the cheese in half and wrap each one in a piece of laminated foil or clear film. The blue moulds should be apparent on the cut faces of the cheeses. The cheeses may be matured at 7°C/45°F for another 3–4 weeks.

Brie and Camembert

The chalky core and mushroomy notes of a young Brie or Camembert soften and gain complexity in flavour as it ripens. This is a cheese that should be enjoyed simply – with bread and a neutral white wine.

There are no significant differences between the recipes for cheese described as Brie, Camembert or Coulommiers. Camembert weighing 250g/10oz often ripens in a slightly different way to a 3kg/13¼lb Brie but this is related to the surface-area-to-volume ratio of the cheese and the impact it has on drainage and mould-ripening rather than any modifications to the basic recipe.

These surface-ripened cheeses owe much of their character to the white mould *Penicillium candidum*, sometimes described as *P. camemberti*. It would be a mistake to think that they rely on this mould alone, however, and that is where a lot of Brie-producers go wrong. Think about the outside of a good French Brie, such as the Brie de Meaux made by Dongé; the white mould is quite thin, even absent in parts, which instead appears ivory and has the 'wrinkly brain' appearance that tells us that yeasts such as *Geotrichum* are at play. Compare that to a run-of-the-mill industrial Brie with its thick layer of white mould that has the texture and the aroma of mushrooms, and an incredibly bitter flavour. The trick to succeeding with this recipe lies with achieving a delicate balance of yeast and moulds; in spite of our apparent familiarity with Brie and Camembert, they can be difficult types to master.

These cheeses are sometimes described as being 'mixed-coagulation', meaning that while the curd is set with rennet rather than by the acidification, the slow drainage of the whey lending their character some of the features of lactic coagulation – namely that the unripe cheeses have a chalky core and the cheese shows differentiation in the degree of ripening between the inner and the outer paste. This can also be a hard thing to balance: if the acidification proceeds faster than the drainage, the cheese will become more lactic in character, over-ripe at the rind but chalky in the middle; if the drainage is faster than the acidification, the cheese can lose too much moisture, becoming firm-textured and dry. ▶

YOU WILL NEED

11.4 litres/3 gallons whole cow's milk

1.0 unit Flora Danica (Christian Hansen) or 0.7 DCU MM100 (Danisco) or equiv. heterofermentative mesophilic starter

0.02 dose DH (Danisco) or equiv. *Debaryomyces hansenii* yeast

0.02 dose GEO17 (Danisco) or equivalent *Geotrichum candidum* yeast

0.03 dose PC42 'VS' or PC53 'Neige' (Danisco) or equivalent *Penicillium candidum* ripening moulds

3.4ml/a little over ⅝ tsp rennet of 1:10,000 strength (or adjusted accordingly, see page 32)

1.8 per cent w/w salt (18g/generous ½oz per 1kg/2¼lb curd)

EQUIPMENT

Large stainless-steel pan; thermometer; wooden spoon; large plastic bucket with lid; pH meter; weighing scales; syringe or small measuring tube; knife; ladle; soft cheese moulds; tray; plastic board; plastic draining mat; plastic container; waxed paper or duplex paper
NB: All equipment should be cleaned and disinfected before use. This cheese can pose a high risk for *Listeria* and other pathogens.

TIME

Production time: 4–6 hours over 24 hours; drying time: 6–12 hours; hastening time: 24 hours; maturation time: 6 weeks

1 Pour the milk into the pan and warm it to 32°C/90°F, stirring occasionally. Remove from the heat when it gets to temperature and pour the milk into the bucket.

2 Measure and thoroughly stir in the starter and ripening culture. Put a lid on the bucket to retain heat and leave the starter to rehydrate for 1 hour.

3 Measure the rennet, then stir it in well for 1 minute before leaving the curd to coagulate for 50 minutes. The first signs should be seen in about 10 minutes but the curd should be left to harden for a further 40 minutes before cutting.

4 Test the curd 50 minutes after renneting (see pages 34–5). It should appear quite firm. Using the knife, make a series of parallel cuts spaced 2.5cm/1in apart, then turn the pan 90 degrees and make more cuts with the same spacing.

5 For the final cut, hold the knife at 45 degrees to the curd and make a series of diagonal cuts. Leave to heal for 5 minutes.

6 Stir the curds gently by hand for 1 minute, then allow them to rest for 4 minutes. The curds will sink very slowly to the bottom of the pan after stirring. Stir and rest the curd six times in total over the course of 30 minutes before letting it settle to the bottom of the pan for the final time.

7 Record the pH of the whey and pour off half of it, being careful not to lose any curd. The curds should be loosely distributed in the whey rather than matted together at the bottom of the pan. At this stage they are still very soft and delicate and care should be taken as they are ladled into moulds positioned in a tray.

8 Using the ladle, divide the curd evenly between the moulds by adding a little to each in rotation. Leave the cheeses in a warm room to drain.

9 After 1 hour, the cheeses will have shrunk down in their moulds and should be firm enough to turn. This can require a quick hand and some confidence. Turn out the cheeses into the palm of your hand, flip them into your other hand, place the mould over the top and quickly turning your hand, neatly drop in the cheese. Those lacking confidence can turn out the cheeses into an empty cheese mould.

10 Turn the cheeses again after 2 hours and then again after 5 hours. Turning the cheese improves the drainage, so long as the turns are not too frequent.

11 The cheese should be ready to unmould 24 hours after cheesemaking began, and have a pH of about 4.80.

12 Measure out 1.8 per cent of the curds' weight in salt. To calculate this, multiply the weight of the cheese in grams by 0.018 to give the weight of salt needed. Sprinkle it evenly on the surface of each cheese.

13 Transfer the cheeses to a plastic board lined with a plastic drainage mat and leave them in an airy room at 20°C/68°F for 6–12 hours until their surfaces start to dry slightly. Turn them once or twice during drying.

14 When the cheeses appear dry on the surface, cover them with an upturned plastic container to retain humidity and leave them in a warm room to hasten for 24 hours to encourage the growth of the yeasts that are essential for the correct rind development. The cheeses should start to look slightly fuzzy and smell yeasty. ▶

15 Turn over the cheeses and transfer them, still covered by the container, to a larder or refrigerator at about 12°C/54°F. Make sure they are spaced closely but evenly on the board to stop the cheeses from sticking together as the moulds grow.

16 Turn over the cheeses every day and remove any condensation that builds up in the container or on the board and draining mat. Wash and sterilize the container, board and mat each week. After a couple of weeks the cheeses should be covered in a thin and even white bloom of *Penicillium candidum*.

17 Remove the container and wrap the cheeses in waxed paper or duplex paper to continue their maturation below 8°C/46°F. Cooling them for a few hours, uncovered, before wrapping will help to prevent condensation from building up inside the packaging but be aware that they will quickly dry out if they are left uncovered for too long.

18 Mature the cheeses below 8°C/46°F for a further 4–6 weeks, according to your preference. During this time, turn them at least every other day until the core starts to become soft.

THE SOFT WATCH

The melting clocks in Salvador Dalí's painting *The Persistence of Memory* are said to have been inspired by the sight of an oozing Camembert, melting in the Catalan sun. Even in cooler climate of Britain, Camembert is normally expected to be served very ripe and runny and the custom is probably a legacy that reflects the length of time it once took to import. In Normandy, the home of Camembert, it can be more common to find the cheese served younger, before it has started to flow freely from the rind, but it's all a matter of personal preference.

Ripened Lactic Cheese

This cheese has a slightly crumbly lactic core with a honeyed, yeasty character imparted by the rind microflora. Depending on the age of the cheese, flavours can be mild and nutty or more intense and goaty, peppery or soapy depending on the milk used.

YOU WILL NEED

11.4 litres/3 gallons whole cow's, goat's or sheep's milk

0.7 unit Flora Danica (Christian Hansen) or equivalent heterofermentative mesophilic starter

0.04 dose GEO17 (Danisco) or equivalent *Geotrichum candidum* yeast

0.01 dose *Penicillium album* ripening moulds (Danisco) (optional: this can be a hard product to source)

1ml/⅕ tsp rennet of 1:10,000 strength (or adjusted accordingly, see page 32)

1.8 per cent w/w salt (18g/generous ½oz per 1kg/2¼lb curd)

EQUIPMENT

Large stainless-steel pan; thermometer; wooden spoon; large plastic bucket with lid; weighing scales; syringe or small measuring tube; pH meter; ladle; lactic-cheese moulds; unvarnished wooden board; plastic draining mat; plastic container; waxed paper or duplex paper

NB: All equipment should be cleaned and disinfected before use. This cheese can pose a high risk for *Listeria* and other pathogens.

TIME

Production time: 3–4 hours over 48 hours; drying time: 12 hours or more; maturation time: at least 2 weeks

Walking past the cheeses on a market stall, my eye is invariably drawn towards the rustic-looking geometric shapes of the ripened lactic cheeses – their rinds wrinkled with white and ivory patches of *Geotrichum* or speckled with moulds such as the grey-green *Penicillium album* that is characteristic of the goat's cheeses of the Loire. From the truncated pyramids of Valençay and the discs of Selles sur Cher to the logs of Sainte-Maure de Touraine with its distinctive straw running down the middle, or the rounded 'horse droppings' of Crottin de Chavignol, there are plenty of cheeses here to inspire the home cheesemaker.

The coagulation of ripened lactic cheese is no different to that of the fresh curds we prepared earlier in the book. To make a good lactic cheese, it is important to ladle the curd as soon as it reaches pH 4.60, when it is at its point of least solubility – also known as the isoelectric point (see page 83). On either side of this point it will prove harder to separate the curds from the whey, resulting in cheeses with an excessive moisture level that tend to become quite sour. Rapid drainage is also important so be careful when ladling since damaged curds do not drain well, and keep the room warm during both coagulation and drainage.

This is not an easy cheese to produce for several reasons. The acidification is long and slow so the milk quality must be exceptional – the delicate flavours betray even the slightest flavour taints; the coagulation temperature is low and only a small amount of rennet is used so cow's milk can be prone to spontaneous creaming or agglutination. The list goes on… Perhaps as a result of the technical difficulties, there are not many cow's-milk lactic cheeses for sale. In France, Saint-Marcellin and Saint Félicien are perhaps the most notable, while in the USA examples include Coupole from Vermont and Larzac made by Fromagerie Monteillet in Washington State. There are a few cheeses made in Britain, such as Golden Cross, Dorstone, and my own one, Little Anne.

When the cream rises on a cow's-milk make, it can drag the starter cultures to the surface, producing a grainy, acidified cream floating on a weak, poorly acidified gel (see Troubleshooting on pages 198–9). Top-stirring the cream until the rennet starts to work can help to reduce the problem but it is important to have stopped stirring before flocculation occurs. This can be a difficult thing to judge. Fortunately, it is not really a problem for goat's milk, which lends itself very well to lactic-cheese technologies.

Faced with all of these problems, the home cheesemaker may well find themselves discouraged from pursuing this recipe. Surely it is just too difficult a cheese to get right? Before you abandon hope, however, consider that I first produced Little Anne, a lactic cheese made from cow's milk, in a bucket in an ordinary kitchen and then matured it on a shelf in the larder. On the basis of the flavour of that prototype cheese, the first commercial batch was sold before it had even been made: testament to the fact that this cheese tastes so good it really is worth the effort involved with making it.

1 Pour the milk into the pan and gently heat it to 21–22°C/70–72°F, stirring continuously with a wooden spoon. Remove from the heat when it gets to temperature and pour the milk into the bucket.

2 Measure and add the starter culture and ripening cultures (yeast and mould, if using) and stir in well.

3 You can add the measured rennet shortly after the starter, but wait at least 10 minutes to allow the starter to rehydrate and disperse in the milk. The coagulation speed and yield of cheese may be improved by allowing the curd to acidify a little before adding the rennet but it should not be added much below pH 6.30.

4 Cover the bucket to keep it warm and leave the mixture to acidify to pH 4.60 over the course of 12–24 hours. The room temperature should be 22–23°C/72–73°F.

5 When the curd reaches pH 4.60, the curd will have shrunk from the sides of the tub releasing a small pool of clear yellow whey, and the curds should have a clean, fresh aroma.

6 Use a small ladle to scoop thin slices of curd and layer them into lactic cheese moulds. The curd is very brittle and great care should be taken to avoid damaging it; rough ladling can result in loss of yield and can impede the drainage.

7 Drain the cheeses over 24 hours at 22–23°C/72–73°F, turning them once or twice. To do so, turn out the cheeses into the palm of your hand, flip them into your other hand, place the mould over the top and quickly turn your hand. The curds will be very delicate at first; a quick hand is required. Those lacking confidence can turn out the cheeses into an empty mould.

8 Leave the cheeses to drain until they have shrunk to about one-third of their initial height.

9 Carefully unmould the cheeses, then turn them out on to a board lined with some plastic mesh.

10 Measure out 1.8 per cent of the curds' weight in salt. To calculate this, multiply the total weight of the cheese in grams by 0.018 to give the weight of salt needed.

11 Sprinkle half of the salt evenly on one side of each cheese. Leave the cheeses at room temperature at 22–23°C/72–73°F for about 6 hours.

12 Turn the cheeses after 6 hours and sprinkle the other side using the remaining weighed-out salt.

13 Leave the cheeses at room temperature at 22–23°C/72–73°F for about another 6 hours. In the conditions usually found in the average home, the cheeses should start to dry slightly on the surface within this time period. They can be left for longer if they are still very wet after 12 hours' drying, but keep an eye on them and take care not to dry them too much, since this causes discolouration and the rinds to crack.

14 Once the cheeses are sufficiently dry, cover them with an upturned plastic container to retain humidity and leave them in a warm room for up to 24 hours more to encourage the growth of yeasts. The cheeses should start to look slightly fuzzy and smell yeasty. Turn the cheeses twice per day.

►

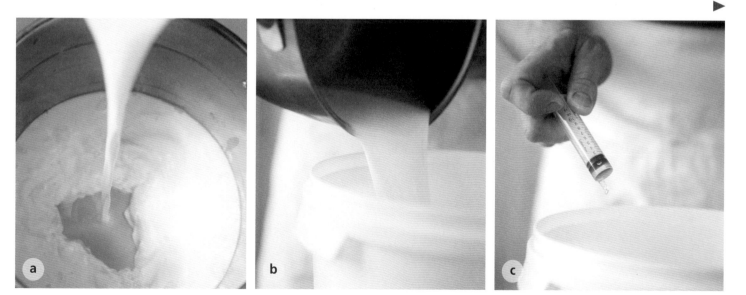

a b c

15 Transfer the cheeses, still covered by the container to retain humidity levels, to a larder or refrigerator at about 12°C/54°F. Make sure they are spaced fairly closely but evenly on the board. They should not be touching.

16 The cheeses can now be matured for several weeks. Turn the cheeses every day and wipe away any condensation that builds up in the container that covers them or on the board and draining mat. Wash and sterilize all of these each week.

17 After 1 week, the cheeses should be slightly wrinkled and may show the first signs of *Penicillium* growth if this was used during their production. Continue to turn them every day, maturing them for at least 2 weeks.

18 The cheeses can be enjoyed nutty and fresh at 2 weeks old, or you can leave them for longer to mature. They will become more strongly flavoured as they age and eventually dry out to become hard little pucks after a few months. These ripened lactic cheeses have a life cycle of their own and there is no 'right' time at which to enjoy them.

19 If keeping the cheeses for longer than 2 weeks, remove the covering container, wrap the cheeses in waxed paper or duplex paper and continue their maturation at 8°C/47°F. Cooling them for a few hours before wrapping them will help to prevent undesirable condensation from building up inside the packaging.

Soft Washed-rind Cheese

The core of soft washed-rind cheese can be yielding and buttery but the rinds offer more robust flavours. For this recipe you can try out different combinations of ingredients and methods to produce textures and rinds with different characters.

There are two approaches to making soft washed-rind cheeses. One is to make a high-moisture cheese following a Brie-style or mixed-coagulation method, with both rennet-set and lactic characteristics and a pH of about 4.80 at unmoulding. The core of these cheeses when under-ripe can appear quite chalky while the area immediately below the rind can soften very quickly, becoming quite runny before the core ripens. Munster and Époisses are two examples of this style of cheese, the rinds of which tend to become very sticky and strong-smelling.

A second type of cheese, illustrated by Livarot and Pont-l'Évêque, is typically at the firmer end of the soft-cheese spectrum and has less of a lactic character. This is achieved by cutting the curd a little finer, stirring it more or by adopting a stabilized-Brie technology – in which a thermophile, *Streptococcus thermophilus*, replaces some of the mesophiles in the starter culture. As the cheeses cool during drainage, the thermophiles stop working and the acidification comes to a halt closer to pH 5.00. These cheeses often show more savoury, meaty flavours.

Like Saint Nectaire (see page 154), Pont-l'Évêque is a mixed-rind cheese, in which the washed-rind bacteria are complemented by white *Penicillium candidum* – a mould most commonly encountered on the surface of Brie and Camembert. Including this mould as part of the process will enable you to produce something akin to a Pont-l'Évêque at home. It is worth trying out the combinations of ingredients and stirring methods as set out below and seeing how they affect the final outcome.

Some cheeses have a small amount of alcohol added to their wash solution – such as Époisses, which is washed in Marc de Bourgogne, a spirit distilled from the grape skins and stems left after wine-making, similar to the Italian Grappa. Others are washed in beer, cider or wine – such as Saint Vernier cheese, which is washed in a Jura wine made from the Savagnin grape. Perhaps I'm a rind-washing purist, but I prefer to wash with salt water and leave flavour development to the microflora of the cheese. Washing cheese in alcohol does not guarantee an incredible flavour but it is worth trying it out for yourself. Do bear in mind that the yeasts that are essential to the rind microflora are sensitive to alcohol, however, so it is best to wash with a solution that is less than 10–12 per cent alcohol by volume (ABV). Beers and ciders fall below this level but many wines and all spirits will exceed it (see box on page 188). ▶

EQUIPMENT

Large stainless-steel pan, plus a lid; thermometer; wooden spoon; pH meter; weighing scales; syringe or small measuring tube; knife; ladle; tray; soft-cheese moulds; lidded plastic container; plastic draining mat; scraps of cheesecloth; waxed paper
NB: All equipment should be cleaned and disinfected before use. This cheese can pose a high risk for *Listeria* and other pathogens.

YOU WILL NEED

11.4 litres/3 US gallons whole cow's milk

0.7 DCU MM100 (Danisco) or heterofermentative mesophilic starter or MA 4001 (Danisco), which includes *Streptococcus thermophilus*

0.02 dose DH (Danisco) or equiv. equivalent *Debaryomyces hansenii*

0.02 dose GEO17 (Danisco) or equiv. *Geotrichum candidum* yeast

0.02 dose BL1 (Christian Hansen) or SR1 (Danisco) or equivalent *Brevibacterium linens* ripening bacteria

0.02 dose PC42 'VS' (Danisco) or equivalent *Penicillium candidum* ripening moulds (optional – for a Pont-l'Évêque-style cheese)

3.3ml/generous ½ tsp rennet of 1:10,000 strength (or adjusted accordingly, see page 32)

1.8 per cent w/w salt (18g/generous ½oz per 1kg/2¼lb curd)

3 per cent salt solution made by adding 30g/1¼oz salt to 1 litre/34fl oz water (NB it is best to make up a small volume of solution each time.)

a glug of beer (ale), for adding to the salt solution for washing the rind (optional)

TIME

Production time: 4–6 hours over 48 hours; maturation time: up to 2 months

1 Pour the milk into the pan and gently heat it to 33°C/91°F, stirring occasionally with a wooden spoon to prevent it sticking. Remove the pan from the heat when the milk gets to temperature and record its pH.

2 Measure out and stir in the starter and ripening culture. Put a lid on the pan to retain heat and leave the starter to rehydrate for 1 hour.

3 Check the temperature of the milk before renneting and, if necessary, heat it back up to 33°C/91°F. Add the rennet and stir it in well for 1 minute, then leave the curd for 50 minutes. The first signs of coagulation should be seen in a little over 10 minutes but the curd should be left for a further 40 minutes before cutting.

4 Test the curd 50 minutes after renneting (see pages 34–5). It should appear quite firm. Using the knife, make a series of parallel cuts spaced 1cm/½in apart, then turn the pan 90 degrees and make a second series of cuts with the same spacing.

5 For the final cut, hold the knife at 45 degrees to the curd and make a series of diagonal cuts. Leave to heal for 5 minutes.

6 Stir the curds gently with a spoon so as to avoid losing too much moisture or causing damage. For a very soft cheese, the curd should be stirred by hand for 1 minute then allowed to settle for 4 minutes. For a slightly firmer cheese, stirring should last for 2 minutes and the curd allowed to settle for 3 minutes. For either type of cheese, this process should be repeated four times over the course of 20 minutes.

7 Stop stirring and allow the curd to settle on the bottom of the pan. This will take up to 5 minutes, with soft-cheese curds settling more slowly than those of the firmer cheeses.

8 Record the pH of the whey and pour off about half of it, being careful not to lose any curd. The curds should be loosely distributed in the remaining whey rather than matted together at the bottom.

9 Ladle out the curd, dividing it equally among the moulds, positioned on a tray. Leave in a warm room to drain.

10 After 1 hour, the cheeses will have shrunk down and should be firm enough to turn. Turn out the cheeses into the palm of your hand, flip them into your other hand, place the mould over the top and quickly turning your hand, neatly drop in the cheese. You can also turn out the cheeses into an empty cheese mould.

11 Turn the cheeses again after 2 hours and again after 5 hours. This improves the drainage, so long as the turns are not too frequent. The cheese should be ready for unmoulding 24 hours after cheesemaking began. The pH should be 5.00 for a firmer cheese or 4.80 for a very soft cheese.

12 Measure out 1.8 per cent of the curds' weight in salt. To calculate this, multiply the total weight of the cheese in grams by 0.018 to give the weight of salt needed. Sprinkle half of the salt evenly on to the upper surface of each cheese and transfer them to the upturned lid of a plastic container lined with plastic drainage mat. Turn after 2–3 hours and salt the other side.

13 Cover with the plastic container and leave at 20°C/68°F for 12–24 hours, until the cheeses start to look slightly fuzzy and smell yeasty. The yeast stage is essential for the correct rind development.

14 Turn over the cheeses and transfer them, still covered by the container, to a larder or refrigerator at about 12°C/54°F. Turn them every other day and wash the rinds by gently rubbing them with a sterilized scrap of new cheesecloth soaked in the salt solution (with the addition of a glug of beer, if using). ▶

e

15 Wipe the cheeses with the salt (and beer, if applicable) solution more often if they start to dry out. Wipe away any condensation that builds up in the container and wash and sterilize it and the mat regularly.

16 The cheese should start to develop a good bacterial smear after 3–4 weeks. Remove the container and wrap the cheeses in waxed paper to continue their maturation below 8°C/46°F. Cooling them for a few hours, uncovered, before wrapping will help to prevent condensation from building up inside the packaging but be aware that they will quickly dry out if left uncovered for too long.

17 The cheeses require no further rind-washing but they should still be turned every few days and used within 3 weeks. Cheeses that were inoculated with *Penicillium* will start to grow a thin coat of white mould while they are wrapped.

WINE- AND SPIRIT-WASHED CHEESES

To calculate how to make up a wash solution if the ABV of your alcohol is greater than 10 per cent:

1 Calculate the volume of alcohol in litres using the equation:

Volume of alcohol = 10 ÷ (ABV -10)

2 Mix this volume of alcohol with 1 litre water.

3 Multiply the combined volume of alcohol and water in litres by 30 to give the number of grams of salt required to make up a 3 per cent solution.

4 Mix this quantity of salt into the alcohol and water mixture. You now have a 10 per cent ABV and 3 per cent salt solution with which to wash the cheeses.

Working example: a cider brandy with an ABV of 42 per cent:

To calculate the volume of alcohol: 10 ÷ (42–10) = 0.3125 litres

So 0.3125 litres of cider brandy is added to 1 litre of water = 1.3125 litres liquid.

To calculate the amount of salt: 1.3125 x 30 = 39.375g

So 39.375g of salt is added to cider brandy and water to give a solution with 3 per cent salt and an ABV of 10 per cent.

Mountain-style Washed-rind Cheese

With a buttery paste, pea-like aroma and firm, slightly elastic texture, this cheese pairs well with rich, potato-based dishes. This recipe requires careful control of temperature and acidification but the luxurious texture of the resulting cheese makes the effort worthwhile.

The semi-hard washed-rind varieties of the Alps make up one of my favourite cheese technologies; silky soft paste with pungent, autumnal aromas from the orange smear on the rind. Fontina, Raclette and Morbier are all at the larger and firmer end of the spectrum while Taleggio, Reblochon and its goat's milk counterpart, Chevrotin, tend to be a little less firm – inhabiting the tasty grey area between the soft and semi-hard cheeses.

All are lightly pressed during drainage and produced using predominantly thermophilic starters – mainly *Streptococcus thermophilus*. The curds are typically cut to the size of rice grains and are not scalded to a high temperature, the temperature of coagulation being worryingly close to 30°C/86°F, below which the thermophiles will not grow. Careful temperature control of the make-room and keeping the cheeses warm while they drain will be critical to achieving a safe acidification profile.

In this recipe, as with that of the Soft Washed-rind Cheese on pages 184–9, I have specified that the ripening cultures, including *Brevibacterium linens*, *Geotrichum candidum* and *Debaryomyces hansenii*, are added to the milk and the cheeses are washed in salt water alone to encourage their growth. An alternative approach would be to add them during ripening by washing the cheeses with a *morge* made up according to the recipe on page 145.

MORBIER-STYLE CHEESE

It is easy to adapt the recipe to produce a cheese based on Morbier, with a layer of activated charcoal running through the middle. This should be 'food-grade' and is often sold as 'cheesemaker's ash'. Make the cheese in the hard cheese mould but at the point of transferring the curd to the mould, divide it into two, covering the base of the mould evenly with half of it. Sprinkle a handful of the ash over the surface of the curd and top up the mould evenly with the remaining curd before continuing to follow the recipe.

YOU WILL NEED

11.4 litres/3 gallons whole cow's or
   goat's milk

0.8 units STB-01 (Christian Hansen)
   or MY800 (Danisco) or equivalent
   thermophilic starter

0.3 units Flora Danica (Christian Hansen)
   or equivalent heterofermentative
   mesophilic starter

0.02 dose DH (Danisco) or an
   equivalent *Debaryomyces hansenii*
   yeast

0.02 dose GEO17 (Danisco) or equivalent
   Geotrichum candidum yeast

0.02 dose BL1 (Christian Hansen)
   or SR1 (Danisco) or equivalent
   Brevibacterium linens ripening
   bacteria

2.9ml/generous ½ tsp of rennet
   1:10,000 strength (or adjusted
   accordingly, see page 32)

1.8 per cent w/w salt (18g/generous ½oz
   per 1kg/2¼lb curd)

3 per cent salt solution made by
   adding 30g/1½oz salt to 1 litre/
   34fl oz water

EQUIPMENT

Large stainless-steel pan, plus a lid;
thermometer; wooden spoon; pH
meter; weighing scales; syringe or
small measuring tube; knife; hand-held
balloon whisk; cheesecloth; moulds:
2 x Reblochon moulds or 5 x Chevrotin
moulds or 1 x 1.5kg/3½lb hard cheese
mould; tray or draining table; ladle;
small weights; unvarnished wooden
board of untreated spruce, pine or
larch; plastic container; waxed paper

TIME

Production time: about 6 hours over
66 hours; maturation time: 2 weeks

We shall follow a process similar to that used for making Reblochon de Savoie, an incredible cheese of which there are many outstanding examples, which is produced by *fermier* cheesemakers in their mountain chalets. These are easily distinguished from the creamery-made cheeses by the presence of a green rather than a red casein disc pressed into the surface of the cheese. Larger cheeses can easily be made by following the same process but pressing the curd in one hard cheese mould rather than several smaller ones.

Vacherin Mont D'Or follows a similar methodology to Reblochon but the curds are cut less finely – to between the size of a walnut and a hazelnut. The resulting soft, moist curds have a plumpness and texture almost reminiscent of marshmallows and the cheeses are not pressed, so they drain more slowly to give a high-moisture cheese that becomes gooey, even spoonable, as it ripens. The cheese becomes so soft in fact that it must be encircled in a *sangle* or band of spruce cambium for support, the wood imparting characteristic phenolic notes to the aroma. Mont D'Or is washed during the early stages of ripening before the moulds begin to grow: in this case *Cylindrocarpon*, since reclassified as a species of *Trichothecium* or *Fusarium*.

Many of these cheeses melt beautifully, with fondue and grilled or broiled Raclette springing immediately to mind, and dishes such as *tartiflette* – in which the humble potato is taken to a level of exquisite indulgence by the addition of bacon, onion and melted Reblochon.

As ever when making cheese, all of the equipment used should be cleaned and especially carefully disinfected before use because these cheeses in particular can pose a high risk for *Listeria* and other pathogens.

1 Pour the milk into the pan and gently heat it to 36–37°C/97–99°F, stirring occasionally with a wooden spoon. Remove from the heat when it gets to temperature. Record the pH of the milk.

2 Measure and then add the starter and ripening culture to the milk and stir in well to combine thoroughly. Put a lid on the pan to retain heat and leave the starter to rehydrate for 1 hour. ▶

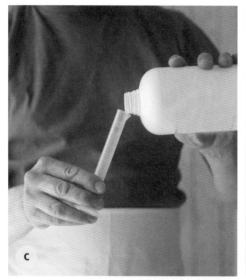

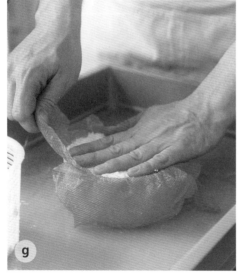

3 Add the rennet and stir it in well for 1 minute before leaving the curd to coagulate for 45 minutes. The first signs of coagulation should be seen about 20 minutes after the addition of the rennet but the curd should be left to firm up for a further 25 minutes before cutting.

4 Test the curd 45 minutes after renneting (see pages 34–5). It should appear firm but soft. Using the sharp knife, make a series of parallel cuts spaced 2.5cm/1in apart, then turn the pan through 90 degrees and make a second series of cuts with the same spacing.

5 For the final cut, hold the knife at 45 degrees to the curd and make a series of diagonal cuts. Leave the curd to heal for 5 minutes.

6 Using the balloon whisk in a gentle stirring motion, cut the curds down to rice-sized grains over 15 minutes, stopping the cut and continuing to stir gently by hand once the curds are at the right size. The grains should start to feel quite dense and will begin to sink more readily to the bottom of the pan.

7 Stop stirring and allow the curd to sink below the yellow-green whey and settle on the bottom of the pan for 5–10 minutes. Prepare the moulds while the curd rests.

8 Warm the moulds and cheesecloth by placing them in a pan of freshly boiled water. Remove from the water, place the moulds side by side in a tray or on a draining table and cover them all with a single sheet of cheesecloth, pressing the cloth down into each mould. Alternatively, you could use individual pieces of cheesecloth for each mould.

9 Measure and then record the pH of the whey and pour it off, being careful not to lose any curd.

10 Carefully divide the curd equally among the moulds using a ladle or an empty mould, then fold over the edges of the cheesecloth to cover the cheeses and keep them warm. The temperature of the curd should be more than 30°C/86°F if the moulds have been sufficiently warmed.

11 Allow the cheeses to drain for about 30 minutes then turn them over in the moulds, covering them up again with the cheesecloth afterwards.

12 Place a circular weight on each cheese – this should be about 1.5kg/3½lb if you are making a larger cheese in the hard cheese mould; 1kg/2/14lb for the Reblochon moulds or 500g/1¼lb for each of the smallest cheeses.

13 After 2 hours, remove the cheeses from the moulds, record the pH of the whey squeezed from the cheesecloth and turn over the cheeses, replacing them into the mould upside down. Replace the weights.

14 When the pH reaches 5.60, remove the cheesecloths, replacing the cheeses back into the moulds directly.

15 Spread out the cheeses to allow them to cool more quickly. Replace the weights and press the cheeses for 12 hours.

16 Unmould the cheeses at the end of this time, by which point the pH should be in the region of 5.10–5.30 and the cheeses should appear soft and elastic.

17 Turn the moulds upside down and place each cheese on top of a mould. ▶

18 Rub the salt into the surface of each cheese and leave it for 2 hours to be mostly absorbed into the cheeses.

19 Transfer the cheeses to a wooden board of untreated spruce, pine or larch, turning them as you do so. Place a plastic container over the cheeses to retain humidity levels and leave them in a warm room at 20°C/68°F to encourage the growth of the yeasts.

20 The cheeses should be turned every day. When the rinds start to look matt (flat) and smell quite yeasty, after about 48 hours, transfer the board, cheeses and container to a cool larder or refrigerator at 12–15°C/54–59°F.

21 Wash the cheeses every other day, each time using a fresh scrap of cheesecloth that has been sterilized in boiling water and then soaked in a 3 per cent salt solution. Wash them more often if they start to dry out. Humidity is very important for the correct ripening of washed-rind cheeses, but the upturned container should prove very effective at creating an appropriate microclimate.

22 When the rind has developed a good bacterial smear after about 2 weeks, cool the cheeses to below 8°C/47°F and wrap them in waxed paper. Under these conditions, the small cheeses should keep for about 1 month, while the larger ones will keep for 1–2 months more.

Troubleshooting

Various problems may be encountered while making cheese, with the causes ranging from the quality and age of the raw milk used through to faulty equipment, contamination, issues with the starter cultures, incorrect storage and, of course, errors in technique.

ACIDIFICATION PROBLEMS

Acidification too fast or pH goes too low

Symptoms: The pH develops too quickly, creating a chalky cheese.

Solution: First, check the calibration of the pH meter, the starter dose and the temperature. If the problem is persistent, the starter dose may be reduced by up to 10 per cent at a time until the correct level is reached for the milk being used. Slow drainage may also cause the pH to drop to low levels. (See 'Fast drainage'.)

Acidification too slow

Symptoms: The pH fails to develop or proceeds more slowly than specified.

Solution: First, check the calibration of the pH meter, the dose of starter used and the temperature of the curd, especially if you are using a thermophilic starter, since these will not grow below 30°C/86°F.

Old or badly stored starter may cause slow acidification, but as long as it has been kept in the freezer its activity should last well beyond the Best Before date.

If the problem persist, it is possible that bacteriophage ('phage') may be responsible, in which case change the starters. A bacteriophage is a virus that infects and kills the starter bacteria. They are strain-specific so switching to an alternative starter should help. Rotate the starters used for different batches of cheese frequently to avoid phage problems.

BRINING PROBLEMS

Slimy rinds on brined cheeses

Symptoms: The rind of a brined cheese becomes soft and slimy.

Solution: It is likely that calcium has been leached from the cheese into the brine. This is especially common with newly made brines. Add 33 per cent calcium chloride solution at a rate of 12.5ml/2½ tsp per 3.79 litres/1 US gallon of brine.

DRAINAGE PROBLEMS

Fast drainage

Symptoms: The curds drain too quickly resulting in a more elastic-textured cheese than desired.

Solution: Cut the curds less finely, stir them less often or less vigorously, and consider reducing the scald temperature slightly.

Slow drainage

Symptoms: The curds drain too slowly, resulting in a more crumbly and less elastic-textured cheese than desired.

Solution: Cut the curds more finely and stir them more often or continuously. Keep the room warm during curd drainage.

GAS PROBLEMS

Large splits or holes in the paste

Symptoms: This is possibly due to late-blowing defect if the cheese variety has a pH above 5.00 at unmoulding, especially if it is accompanied by off-flavours. At low levels this may not be entirely unpleasant.

Solution: Ensure the salt level is correct, consider the use of lysozyme (if available) and avoid milk made from silage-fed animals. Avoid making high-pH hard and semi-hard cheeses if the problem persists.

Tiny pinprick holes in the paste

Symptoms: Coliforms, such as *E.coli*, which may be introduced by contaminated milk or equipment, will produce lots of tiny holes in the paste of the cheese – usually visible at unmoulding.

Solution: Wash and disinfect the equipment and review the milk supply.

MOZZARELLA AND *PASTA FILATA* PROBLEMS

Curd does not stretch

Symptoms: The curd does not stretch after it has been milled and salted.

Solution: Check the pH of the curd – it should be about 5.20. The curd's ability to melt and stretch is highly pH-dependent, which means that better control of the acidification is required.

Mozzarella doesn't melt

Cause: Incorrect pH or insufficient heat.

Solution: Monitor the pH and make sure it is close to 5.20 at the point of stretching the curd. Ensure that the water is hot enough to cause it to melt.

RIND PROBLEMS

Undesirable black or grey mould

Symptoms: *Mucor* is a grey/brown mould often found on tomme-style cheeses but which can be a spoilage mould on soft cheese, where it is associated with bitter flavours. It likes low-salt, high-moisture conditions and cool temperatures (below 10°C/50°F).

Solution: Make sure drainage is satisfactory, salt is applied evenly and the hastening (if appropriate) is carried out at the correct temperature.

Clean and disinfect the equipment carefully to eradicate the moulds since they can become a persistent problem.

Other undesirable moulds
Symptoms: These may be expected on the surface of a natural-rind cheese such as tomme or Cheddar.
Solution: Ensure that the cheese is matured below 15°C/59°F to avoid the formation of mycotoxins. Otherwise, remove the cheese and clean and disinfect equipment to avoid further contamination.

Cheese mites
Symptoms: Mites burrow into the surface of the cheese and produce a distinctive brown dust. These are most common on longer-aged cheeses with a natural mould rind and on Cheddar and the territorial-style cheeses.
Solution: Brush off the mites and mould each week during turning and remove the brushings, throwing them away or burning them as soon as possible to help to control the mite population.

Glow-in-the-dark rinds (or fluorescent residues on equipment)
Symptoms: *Pseudomonas fluorescens* is a spoilage bacteria present in raw milk or as a post-pasteurization contaminant in pasteurized milk. It may also be present as an environmental contaminant. It can produce a pigment that is fluorescent under UV light and is associated with bitterness in the cheese. It is usually found on soft cheeses, especially ones with washed rinds.
Solution: Carefully clean and disinfect the equipment to eradicate the bacteria and consider changing or heat-treating the milk supply.

Dry or cracked rind
Symptoms: The rind appears dry on the outside or cracks appear on its surface.

Solution: Humidity during storage is too low. Cover the cheeses with an upturned plastic container to maintain humidity.

Slipping rind
Symptoms: The rind separates from the core of the cheese.
Solution: Acidification may be too fast or drainage too slow. This should be treated as an acidification or drainage problem. Alternatively, the hastening time or temperature may be too long or too high.

Washed rinds do not develop
Symptoms: Nothing much happens as the cheese matures.
Solution: Ensure cheese is stored in humid conditions at the correct temperature and that hastening was carried out at the right temperature. Wash more frequently to establish the surface smear.

Cheese is too 'wrinkly'
Symptoms: Excessive growth of yeasts including *Geotrichum*.
Solution: Reduce the dose of yeast and the length of time in the hastener or the temperature of hastening. Yeasty, slipping rinds may sometimes be a result of an acidification defect.

White rind is too thick
Symptoms: Excessive growth of *Penicillium* on a mould-ripened cheese – often associated with a bitter-tasting rind.
Solution: Reduce the dose of *Penicillium* or switch to a different strain. Increase the dose of yeasts such as *Geotrichum* or *Debaryomyces*.

TEMPERATURE-CONTROL PROBLEMS
Curd cooling too quickly
Solution: Increase the room temperature and cover the cheeses or curds.

Curds cooling too slowly
Solution: Reduce the temperature of the room, uncover and spread out the curds (for territorial-style cheese such as Cheddar) or the cheeses themselves (for thermophilic hard or semi-hard cheeses).

FLAVOUR DEFECTS
Sour yogurt
Cause: The yogurt has been incubated for too long or at too high a temperature.
Solution: Monitor the pH during acidification. To control post-acidification, ferment the yogurt below 45°C/113°F and use a lower dose of *Lactobacillus* to *Streptococcus* in the starter.

Bitter cheese
Cause: Bitterness is often related to incomplete proteolysis, ie the caseins have been broken down to bitter peptides faster than they can be turned into amino acids. It is often associated with the growth of *Pseudomonas, Mucor* and *Penicillium;* use of vegetarian rennet or high doses of rennet; excess starter culture; lack of diversity in the ripening microflora; use of low-sodium salts; or the wrong dose of salt.
Solution: Reduce dose of rennet or starter culture; increase salt level if deficient; and improve drainage of curd if overly wet.

Soapy and rancid flavours
Cause: Increased lipolysis can cause soapy, peppery, sweaty and other rancid flavours. This may be caused by damage to the milk fat-globule's membrane due to agitation of the milk; the presence of *Pseudomonas;* or an excessive dose of lipase enzymes.
Solution: Reduce the dose of lipase enzymes, if used; clean and disinfect equipment if spoilage organisms are suspected to be responsible; and review the milk supply if the problem persists.

Glossary

Affineur This person is responsible for the careful maturation of cheese after production, ensuring that the conditions are right for its proper flavour development, before distributing it.

Bac de caillage A coagulation tub used for the production of lactic cheeses in France. Strong, lidded, non-brittle food-grade plastic containers with a capacity of 15–20 litres/4–5.25 US gallons can be substituted by the home cheesemaker.

Brining The salting of a cheese by immersing it in a saturated salt solution, as is common with the production of Gouda and Parmigiano Reggiano.

Casein The principal protein in milk, making up about 80 per cent of the total protein, the remainder being whey protein.

Cheddaring Blocking and stacking the curd during the production of Cheddar cheese to improve drainage while the acidification takes place. Cheddaring is followed by milling and dry-salting.

Cheese iron A device that is used for extracting and inspecting a sample of hard or blue cheese during its maturation, without cutting it open.

Curd mill A peg mill or chip mill used to break up curds before they are salted and moulded. Small quantities of curd may be milled by hand.

Cutting the curd Slicing the curd into small pieces after coagulation to increase the surface area and encourage whey loss.

Direct acidification The addition of an acid to milk to reduce the pH, rather than achieving a pH drop through the use of cultures.

Direct Vat Inoculation (DVI) starters Freeze-dried cultures intended to be added directly to the milk.

Flocculation The first sign of coagulation after renneting the milk, when micelles bond together. The point at which the liquid becomes a weak gel.

Follower A lid for a cheese mould.

Hardening The process of coagulation after rennet has been added to milk. The longer hardening goes on, the stronger the bonds between the micelles and the less whey can be drained from the curd.

Hastening The period in which a mould-ripened or washed-rind cheese is held in a warm room at a high humidity in order to encourage the growth of yeasts that are important to the ripening process.

Heterofermentative Lactic acid bacteria that produce a mixture of lactic acid, gas and aroma compounds.

Homofermentative Lactic acid bacteria that produce lactic acid but not gas or aroma compounds.

Lactic acid bacteria (LAB) Bacteria that ferment the lactose in milk into lactic acid. These may be deliberately added as a starter culture (SLAB) or present as accidental contaminants (non-starter LAB or NSLAB).

Lactic coagulation The coagulation of the milk by the acidification caused by lactic acid bacteria.

Larding The application of lard to the rind of a territorial cheese. Lard is used to stick on the cloth binding during the coating of the cheese.

Late-blowing defect Also known as butyric acid fermentation, this defect is caused by the presence of *Clostridium* species in the milk and results in cracks and splits in the rind of the finished cheese, along with an unpleasant smell and rancid flavour.

Lipolysis The process of fat breakdown that plays a part in the flavour development of some cheeses.

Mesophile Bacteria such as *Lactococcus lactis* that typically grow optimally at temperatures between 20–40°C/68–104°F but can also grow in conditions as low as 10°C/50°F.

Micelles Small units of casein, from which protrude hydrophilic kappa-casein tails.

Milkstone A white scaly deposit found on cheese moulds caused by hard water. It can be removed using an acid product, such as vinegar or hydrochloric acid.

Milling The breaking up of the curd either by chopping, tearing or passing through a curd mill.

Mixed coagulation A cheese that shows characteristics of being both lactic- and rennet-coagulated. Examples include Brie and Camembert, which are rennet-set but drain slowly, reaching a low final pH.

Mixed rind A cheese ripened by both rind-washing and mould growth.

Morge The smear solution used in the ripening of washed-rind cheeses, consisting of a weak salt solution populated by yeasts and bacterial cultures.

Mould (US mold) A multicellular fungus that grows by means of a thread-like network of cells called a mycelium. Examples include *Penicillium*, *Fusarium*, *Scopulariopsis* and *Mucor*.

Mould-ripened A cheese that is ripened by moulds either internally (blue cheese) or externally (Camembert).

Pasteurized milk This is milk that has been heated to a temperature of 72°C/161°F for 15 seconds or, less commonly, to 63°C/145°F for 30 minutes.

Pathogen A microbe capable of causing disease, such as *Listeria*, *Campylobacter* or *Salmonella*.

Peptide A compound comprising two or more amino acids. These are formed during proteolysis and can cause bitterness in cheese.

Piercing In blue-cheese production, sterilized needles or skewers are used to pierce the cheese during the maturation phase in order to allow oxygen to reach the blue moulds, since this is required for their growth and pigmentation.

Proteolysis The process by which casein begins to break down into long and intermediate peptides, then shorter peptides, and finally amino acids, which are the precursor to many of the flavour compounds we find in mature cheeses. Proteolysis is carried out by natural milk enzymes, such as plasmin, as well as retained rennet, the enzymes of LAB and those of the ripening cultures.

Psychrotrophic bacteria These cold-tolerant bacteria can be grown at temperatures as cold as 4°C/39°F.

Raw milk This is milk that has not been heated at source above 40°C/104°F.

Relative Humidity (RH) The level of water vapour in air expressed as a percentage of the amount needed for saturation at the same temperature.

Rennet Traditionally an enzyme from the stomach of a calf, kid or lamb used to coagulate milk. Vegetarian, vegetable and recombinant rennet can also be used.

Renneting The point at which rennet is added to the milk.

Scalding Heating the curds after cutting and before moulding to encourage them to express whey. Used in the production of hard cheeses.

Smear-Ripened See Washed-rind entry.

Sodium hypochlorite (bleach) This is used for disinfecting equipment.

Spoilage organisms A yeast, mould or bacteria that is not harmful but that is undesirable on a particular food as it impairs the flavour or appearance. Examples include yeast in yogurt, *Mucor* on the rind of a Camembert and *Pseudomonas* in milk, cheese and butter. *Mucor* on the rind of tomme would not be considered to be a spoilage organism.

Territorial cheeses A name given to the traditional regional cheeses of Great Britain, which include Cheddar, Cheshire and Lancashire.

Thermized milk This is unpasteurized milk that is heat-treated to 63°C/145°F for 15 seconds to control spoilage organisms before cheesemaking.

Thermophile Bacteria like *Streptococcus thermophilus* that require temperatures to be above 30°C/86°F for them to grow.

Titratable acidity Determining the lactic acid content of a sample of whey or milk by reacting it with sodium hydroxide in the presence of phenolphthalein indicator. This method is used by the makers of Territorial cheeses but this book instead concentrates on the measurement of pH.

Washed-rind A cheese in which the rind is washed in a solution that may contain salt water or alcohol to encourage the growth of sticky orange bacteria on the surface of the cheese.

Whey The yellow-green liquid that separates from the curd after the coagulation process. It is composed of water and whey proteins.

Whey protein The component of the milk protein that remains in the whey after coagulation and that is extracted during the production of ricotta.

Yeast A unicellular organism belonging to the fungi kingdom, such as *Debaryomyces*, *Geotrichum* or *Kluyveromyces*.

Acknowledgements

The author would like to thank his wife, Hannah Roche, for proofing his first drafts, and the photographer William Shaw for such an efficient and enjoyable shoot. In addition, the author and publisher would like to thank the following establishments for permitting them to take photographs on their premises and for all their help:

La Fromagerie

Patricia Michelson opened her first store in Highbury, North London in 1992 and a second one on Moxton Street (pictured), near Marylebone High Street, 10 years later. The stores, with their famed walk-in cheese-rooms, are packed from floor to ceiling with delicious and exotic cheeses from every corner of Europe, carefully selected and all ripened to perfection by La Fromagerie's own *affineurs*. www.lafromagerie.co.uk

Paxton and Whitfield

Paxton and Whitfield can trace their history back to 1742. Having been awarded a Royal Warrant of Appointment to HM Queen Victoria in 1850 and moved into their flagship store at 93 Jermyn Street in 1896, Paxton's have weathered over 200 years of ups and downs in the market. This remarkable feat has been achieved in no small part as a result of their policy of stocking high-quality cheeses sourced from the best producers and sold in peak condition. www.paxtonandwhitfield.co.uk

Nettlebed Creamery

Founded by Rose Grimond in 2015, Nettlebed is one of a new generation of producers participating in the continued revival of traditional cheesemaking practices. They produce a modern British cheese, St Bartholomew, from organic raw milk sourced from a single herd at nearby Merrimoles Farm Dairy. www.nettlebedcreamery.com

Brockhall Farm

Sarah Hampton's herd of beautiful pedigree pure Saanen goats are the focus at Brockhall Farm and the attention she pays to their happiness and well-being is rewarded with milk of incredible quality and flavour. Cheesemaking here is very much a labour of love driven by great respect for the animals producing the milk. The dairy produces a range of cheeses including fresh, soft and semi-hard varieties made from raw goat's milk. www.brockhallfarm.com

Mr Moyden's Handmade Cheese

Husband-and-wife team Martin and Beth Moyden make several varieties of hard and blue raw-milk cheese near Market Drayton, Shropshire, using milk from a nearby farm. Their hands-on approach to cheesemaking and attention to detail produces cheeses of great consistency and quality, which they resolutely refuse to compromise in order to satisfy growing demand. www.mrmoyden.com

Suppliers

A number of online suppliers of cheesemaking equipment and some of the key ingredients will deliver internationally; check the terms and conditions of delivery on the individual supplier's website for full details. Cookware stores also stock some of the equipment required, such as pans, knives, cheesecloths, whisks, thermometers, and other general utensils.

UK
Ascott Dairy
+44 (0)1626 880 894
www.ascott-dairy.co.uk/dairy

The Cheese Making Shop
+44 (0)121 744 4844
www.cheesemakingshop.co.uk

Goat Nutrition Ltd.
+44 (0)1233 770 780
www.gnltd.co.uk

Jongia (UK) Ltd.
+44 (0)121 744 4844
www.cheesemakingshop.co.uk

Moorlands Cheesemakers Ltd.
+44 (0)1963 350 634
www.cheesemaking.co.uk

USA
Artisan Geek
+1 212 500 0590
artisangeek.com

Get Culture
+1 608 268 0462
www.getculture.com

New England CheeseMaking Supply Co.
+1 413 397 2012
www.cheesemaking.com

TheCheeseMaker.com
+1 414 745 5483
www.thecheesemaker.com

CANADA
Fromagex
+1 866 437 6624
www.fromagex.com

Make Cheese
+1 403 689 3552
www.makecheese.ca

AUSTRALIA AND NEW ZEALAND
Cheese Links
+61 3 5282 1984
www.cheeselinks.com.au

Curds & Whey
+64 9 376 3055
www.curdsandwhey.co.nz

Omnom
+61 (0)47 678 7267
www.omnomcheese.com

Index

For Mike & Judy Smales

This edition is published by Lorenz Books
an imprint of Anness Publishing Ltd
info@anness.com
www.lorenzbooks.com
www.annesspublishing.com

© Anness Publishing Ltd 2022

PUBLISHER: Joanna Lorenz
SENIOR EDITOR: Lucy Doncaster
DESIGNER: Adelle Mahoney
PHOTOGRAPHY: William Shaw
PROP STYLING: Jenny Iggleden
PRODUCTION CONTROLLER: Ben Worley

PUBLISHER'S CREDITS
• Thanks to Maddocks Farm Organics for the edible flowers used for the Gruyère recipe and The Courtyard Dairy for the use of the Caerphilly image on p130.
• Picture credits: Alamy p13, p17, p130; iStock p23, p25l, p26, p28, p35r, p154b; Paul Thomas p34, p153b.

IMPORTANT NOTES

ABOUT THE AUTHOR

Having graduated with a degree in biochemistry in 1999, Paul Thomas worked for several years as an affineur at respected cheesemonger, IJ Mellis in Edinburgh. He then spent six years as head cheesemaker at Lyburn Farm in the New Forest, where he hand-made many cheeses, including the award-winning Old Winchester (US: Old Smales) and Stoney Cross, and helped to develop the washed-rind cheeses Little Colonel and Francis in association with James's Cheese. He set up Thimble Cheesemakers in 2013, making soft raw-milk cheeses such as Little Anne and Dorothy, before setting up Paul Thomas Dairy Consultancy & Training to provide technical support to farmhouse and artisan dairy producers.

As well as teaching at The School of Artisan Food and the River Cottage Cookery School, Paul helps cheesemakers around the world, both in person and via webinar-based sessions, to address issues such as product development, troubleshooting defects, dairy hygiene and the biochemistry of flavour development. He delivers training to food enforcement officers on food safety in relation to cheesemaking and he is one of five technical experts writing the European Guide to Good Hygiene Practices for Farmhouse and Artisan Cheesemakers.